WITHDRAWN

# POETRY AND REVOLUTION IN RUSSIA 1905-1930

**AN EXHIBITION OF BOOKS AND MANUSCRIPTS**

PREPARED BY LAZAR FLEISHMAN

■ OCTOBER 16, 1988
TO JANUARY 6, 1989
LOUIS R LURIE ROTUNDA
CECIL H GREEN LIBRARY

**STANFORD UNIVERSITY LIBRARIES**          STANFORD, CALIFORNIA 1989

Designed by Peter Rutledge Koch and, through the kind offices of Adobe Systems and Sumner Stone, set in Adobe Garamond and Futura types with the assistance of Fred Brady and Margery Cantor. Cover produced with Adobe Illustrator 88 by Fred Brady.

Copyright 1989 by the Board of Trustees of the Leland Stanford Junior University
ISBN 0-911221-10-7

# PREFACE

The University Libraries have long wanted to do an exhibit which would give expression to aspects of their extensive Slavic collections. While the holdings of the Hoover Institution are well known, those of the University Libraries are less so. Yet the two libraries complement each other nicely. Where the Hoover has tended to focus on Russian politics and society in the twentieth century, the Libraries have concentrated on documenting the traditions of the arts and literature in Russia. Invariably, however, such distinctions become blurred, and the present exhibition is a good example of how and why this happens. If it is generally difficult to approach literature outside of its social and political context, it is impossible in the case of Russia, where the status of the writer and the power of the word have enjoyed a prestige that binds art to politics in ways not true in the West. Thus, while the exhibit draws primarily on the rich holdings of Russian literature in the University Libraries, it also incorporates selected items from the Hoover. We appreciate the willingness of Charles Palm, the Associate Director of the Hoover, to allow us to borrow material for the show.

The story of the origins and growth of Stanford's Slavic collections has been admirably told by Wojciech Zalewski, Curator of Slavic Collections, in his recent monograph, *Slavica Collections at Stanford University*. But it is worth recalling here that many of the items on display in the exhibit go back to the earliest moments of that story, when Frank Golder of the History Department travelled to Europe and Russia in the 1920s on behalf of Herbert Hoover and the American Relief Administration. Literature was not Golder's top priority, but his friendship with Henry Lanz, Stanford's first professor of Slavic literature, made it a difficult category to ignore. However, it was not until relatively recently that the Libraries began systematically building their Russian literature collections. Two major acquisitions stand out with special prominence and figure largely in this exhibit: one, which brought to Stanford several hundred volumes of poetry from the collection of Alexandre Benois, and the other, which moved the extraordinary library of Professor Gleb Struve of Berkeley down to this end of the San Francisco Bay.

Neither the development of the collections nor this exhibit would have been possible without the keen interest of the Slavic Department at Stanford. Since his arrival on campus three years ago, Lazar Fleishman has been especially attentive to the state of the collections in Russian literature, and his interests are handsomely reflected in the present exhibit. The Libraries are deeply grateful to Professor Fleishman for his enthusiastic collaboration in our shared enterprise.

Staff of the Libraries brought their own expertise to bear on the shaping and production of the exhibit and catalogue. Mark Dimunation, Steven McCarthy, and Autumn Stanley did their customary fine work, while Wojciech Zalewski was helpful with the citations. The Libraries are once again indebted to William Glikbarg of Los Angeles for his unflagging support of our exhibit publications program.

MICHAEL T. RYAN
*Frances and Charles Field Curator*
*of Special Collections*

# INTRODUCTION

Winds of renewal and radical change swept all areas of Russian culture during the turbulent years between 1905 and 1930. Lyric poetry was particularly affected. Except for the age of Pushkin (the first third of the nineteenth century), never before or since has poetry played so central a role in the Russian cultural scene, or undergone such transformations. Its rapid and profound evolution during these two and a half decades is reflected in a spate of literary schools and trends with conflicting aesthetic platforms and diverse artistic directions. As Osip Mandelstam put it in his article "Attack," published in *Russia* in 1924, "The rapid change in poetic schools in Russia has sent the reader reeling."

Often called the Silver Age of Russian poetry, this volatile period produced a constellation of lyric poets: Aleksandr Blok, Vladimir Mayakovsky, Boris Pasternak, Marina Tsvetaeva, Andrey Bely, Velemir Khlebnikov, Anna Akhmatova, Osip Mandelstam, Nikolay Gumilev, Ivan Bunin and Vladislav Khodasevich. No Russian reader, of course, would rank any one of them with Pushkin, whose career marks the so-called Golden Age in Russian poetry. Yet in variety of poetic styles and intensity of artistic experimentation, the modernist period far surpassed that earlier flowering of Russian poetry, also called the Romantic age.

Russian lyric poetry of the early twentieth century—like Russian painting, theater, ballet, and music of the same period—gained wide recognition abroad. Some contemporary observers even claimed that in stylistic diversity, lyrical power, and boldness, it was the most interesting poetry in Europe. Though such assertions can hardly be proven, they are noteworthy, if only because no such claims have ever been made for any other period of Russian poetry. To a large extent this reputation and influence stemmed from poetry's intimate relationship with those social and intellectual forces which brought about the Revolution. Some participants in the Russian cultural revival of the early twentieth century prophesied unheard-of social cataclysms and transformations—global wars, bloody revolutions, even, as in a Bely poem of 1918, the creation of the atomic bomb. Others were directly involved in the propaganda or underground political activities of revolutionary parties. Such was the case with Konstantin Balmont, first among the Russian Symbolist poets to achieve wide popular fame, and with Vladimir Mayakovsky, the greatest poet of Russian Futurism. But even writers who tried to remain aloof from social and political issues were inevitably touched by the Revolution. It is therefore impossible to understand the works of these poets, to say nothing of Russian culture at this period, outside this apocalyptic context.

In 1917 some of the leading poets—Blok, Bely, and Mayakovsky among them—enthusiastically welcomed the Revolution. Others—such as Nikolay Gumilev or Marina Tsvetaeva—just as passionately rejected it. The Revolution had a tremendous, even tragic impact on the destiny and poetry of both groups. The nascent Soviet state became increasingly intolerant toward any manifestation of artistic independence. By the early 1920s Russian culture had split into two parallel but relatively autonomous parts, the Soviet and the émigré. Though each experienced the decline of Silver Age literature, that decline took different forms and had different causes in the two milieux. In Soviet Russia it resulted from direct pressure from the State; in exile, it occurred as an organic process. The death of Vladimir Mayakovsky in 1930 marked the demise of the literary avant-garde in Russia and coincided with the imposition of the Stalinist dictatorship in all spheres of intellectual life. The brief flowering of Russian poetry came to an end.

The combined holdings of the Stanford University Libraries and the Hoover Institution form one of the world's finest collections of twentieth-century Russian literature and history. They enable us to discover the connections between various seemingly unrelated phenomena of cultural and political life. For the present exhibition, I have selected over a hundred original printed and manuscript materials to adumbrate the history of Russian poetry during the period in question. My goal is to show all major poetic schools of that time with their leading representatives, as well as some minor and lesser-known poets who illuminate fundamental features of the epoch.

The exhibit opens with poets who began work on the eve of the First Russian Revolution (1905-1907) and closes with 1930. Thus, it encompasses the first World War, the February and Bolshevik revolutions of 1917, the Russian Civil War and its aftermath.

I would like to dedicate this exhibit to the memory of three men who, themselves offspring of the Silver Age and witnesses of revolutionary storms in Russia, have promoted the study of Russian culture in the San Francisco Bay Area in various ways. These are Henry Lanz (1886-1945), founder of the Slavic Department at Stanford; Boris I. Nikolaevsky (1887-1966), whose collection at the Hoover Institution has no equal; and Gleb Struve (1898-1985), former Professor of Russian Literature at the University of California at Berkeley, whose pathbreaking works on twentieth-century Russian literature have served as a model for generations of scholars.

LAZAR FLEISHMAN
*Professor of Russian Literature*
*Department of Slavic Languages and Literature*
*Stanford University*
*October 1988*

# THE NEW SYMBOLISM

The literary debuts of Aleksandr Blok (1880-1921) and Andrey Bely (1880-1934) in 1902-03 marked a decisive new stage in Russian poetry. In contrast to the first generation of Symbolists, the "Decadents," who entered the literary scene in the mid-1890s with slogans of extreme individualism and aestheticism, the younger poets preached active involvement in the imminent transformation of the social order, indeed of the entire universe. Drawing on the teachings of the philosopher-poet Vladimir Soloviev (1853-1900), they prophesied the Apocalypse, the end of history. The new universe would emerge only as a result of world cataclysms. The "Eternal Feminine" would appear, bringing spiritual rebirth and destroying the world's evil.

The main representatives of this second stage of the Symbolist movement were Blok, Bely, and Vyacheslav Ivanov (1866-1949). All three were ardent followers of Vladimir Soloviev. For them "Symbolism" was not just a literary movement, but rather a new spirit of the times; their principal concern was not art, but "contemporary man's soul." The atmosphere of mystical revelation and tense expectations of impending world transformation profoundly influenced their poetic style and world view.

## ■ THE ARGONAUTS

In 1903, the young Solovievans formed a circle called the "Argonauts." This was a group of Moscow University students who joined together to pursue the new goals for art. However, it was not just a literary circle: only three of the participants—Bely, Sergey Soloviev and Ellis (Lev Kobylinsky)—later became writers. They likened their aspirations to the quest for the Golden Fleece. The driving force behind the circle, and its dominant figure, was Bely. The Argonauts' theoretical platform was never clearly formulated and remained rather vaguely reported in later memoirs. But many references to their ideas can be found in the early lyrics of Bely's first collection of verses, *Gold in Azure*. [1]

Both the book's title and its opening poems reflect the extraordinary role of solar imagery in the poetic mythology of the group. As Bely wrote to Émile Medtner on April 19, 1903: "My desire for the Sun is growing stronger. I feel like dashing through the black void and sailing through

**1** ANDREY BELY.
*Zoloto v lazuri* (Gold in Azure).
Moscow, 1904.

the ocean of stagnation. But how can I overpower the void?" The Argonauts called for *zhiznetvorchestvo* (life-creation) as their ultimate goal in art. This directly contradicted the Decadents' theories of art for art's sake. As opposed to the traditional concept of the artist producing works of art, the Argonauts saw as their ultimate mission a complete transformation of the universe. The group promulgated the idea of the artist as "theurgist"-social alchemist and transformer—or priest. This concept acquired distinctly eschatological overtones and later played a central role in the aesthetics of Russian Symbolism. As early as the First Russian Revolution of 1905, the Argonauts came to realize the illusory character of their "desire for the Sun." The mournful notes of disillusionment with the theurgical conception of art can already be heard in *Gold in Azure*. The Argonaut "brotherhood" soon disintegrated, but its ideas persisted. Indeed, as Bely saw it, the Argonauts set forth the ideals later embraced and embodied by the Symbolists.

The solar symbolism of *Gold in Azure* echoed the themes in *Let Us Be Like the Sun: The Book of Symbols* by Konstantin Balmont (1867-1942), one of the founders of the Decadent movement in the 1890s. [2] These poems, appearing in 1903, just before *Gold in Azure*, brought the author wide recognition. It was not by chance that the opening poems in Bely's collection were dedicated to Balmont and represented a kind of dialogue with the latter's poetry.

In his review of *Let Us Be Like the Sun*, Valery Briusov found in Balmont a "poet of the new art," in which the "tremor of the future manifested itself so patently." "Perhaps others will recognize more clearly the whole secret meaning of the age, but rarely does anyone more than Balmont carry this age within himself,…or experience it more fully. Balmont is first and foremost a 'New Man'; he has a new soul, new passions, ideals and aspirations, all different from those of previous generations." In Briusov's mind, Balmont's place in literature was unquestionable: "All of his contemporaries are forced to take care…lest they fall into his field of attraction. To wrestle with Balmont in the field of pure lyric is a dangerous feat." [3]

The 1905 Revolution brought sudden changes in Balmont's life and his literary status as a leading Decadent poet. He had joined the Social-Democrats abroad and in 1906 published in Paris his collection of revolutionary lyrics, *Songs of an Avenger*. [4, 5] Because of this publication he was forbidden to return to Russia until the 1913 amnesty. These propagandist verses marked the decline of Balmont's poetry both in quality and, ironically, since they were addressed for the first time to a wider public, in influence on contemporary audiences.

Andrey Bely was the penname of Boris Bugaev; "Bely" (white) alludes to the eschatological meaning of the color white in the Apocalypse. He was born in 1880 to the family of the prominent Russian mathematician Nikolai Bugaev, Professor and Dean of Faculty for Physics and Mathematics of Moscow University. His family background and academic acquaintances early awakened in Bely a strong interest in science. Between 1899 and 1903 he took various courses in the natural sciences at Moscow University and after graduation reenrolled in the University to study philology and philosophy. Bely met Vladimir Soloviev in spring 1900 in Moscow and had an inspiring talk with him.

Bely's first publications appeared during his university years: his prose work *Symphony*—one of four "Symphonies"—and his first articles in *The World of Art* were published in 1902. [6, 7] *The World of Art*, the earliest magazine of Russian modernist artists, was founded in Petersburg in

**2** KONSTANTIN BALMONT.
"Budem kak solntse: Kniga simvolov" (Let Us Be Like the Sun: The Book of Symbols) in *Polnoe sobranie sochinenii* (Collected Works). Moscow, 1912.

**3** VALERY BRIUSOV.
"Balmont" in *Mir iskusstva* (World of Art), 1903:7.

On loan from The Hoover Institution

**4** *Krasnoe znamia* (Red Banner). 1906:1 (May).

On loan from The Hoover Institution

"Songs of an Avenger" first appeared in this revolutionary émigré monthly magazine which was published in Paris by Aleksandr Amfiteatrov. It sought the overthrow of monarchy and the establishment of the "All-Russian Federative Republic." Among its contributors were Balmont and Maksimilian Voloshin.

**5** KONSTANTIN BALMONT.
*Pesni mstitelia* (Songs of an Avenger). Paris, 1907.

On loan from The Hoover Institution

Open to the poem "Nikolaiu Poslednemu" (To Nicholas the Last), the present copy belonged to Feliks Vadimovich Volkhovskoy (1846-1914), a famous Russian revolutionary. With the aid of George Kennan, Volkhovskoy fled from Siberia abroad and settled in London in 1890. One of the founders of the party of Socialist-Revolutionaries, he was also a writer. A book of his poems appeared in Moscow in 1907.

**6** ANDREY BELY.
"Pevitsa" (The Singer) in *Mir iskusstva* (The World of Art), 1902:11.

On loan from The Hoover Institution

"Our age is a special one: we recalled the mysteries which have gripped us from time immemorial. They never change. Invisible discoveries have begun: they are bursting into our life, breaking its barriers.…Great times are coming.…Greatness bursts from the chest. People are becoming symbols—they are becoming deeper."

**7** ANDREY BELY.
"Formy iskusstva" (The Forms of Art) in *Mir iskusstva* (The World of Art), 1902:12.

On loan from The Hoover Institution

In this outline of his systematic aesthetic theory, Bely advanced the idea of the Mysterium, which would replace all traditional art forms. It later gave impetus to the artistic quest of the composer Alexandre Scriabine and had tremendous impact on the second-generation Symbolists' literary work. Blok described the article as "a revelation." "It is the 'song of the system' which I have long awaited."

1898 by Alexandre Benois and Serge Diaghilev and lasted until December 1904. It aimed slogans of artistic freedom against the traditions of academism and social utility dominating Russian art in the second half of the nineteenth century, and opened its pages to Symbolist criticism. Among its patrons was Tsar Nicholas II, who agreed to subsidize it in response to Valentin Serov's request.

Bely made his poetic debut the next year in the Symbolist miscellanies *Griffon* and *Northern Flowers*. He was the most prolific of the Russian Symbolists. Besides poetry he wrote novels and introduced new prose forms that have won him an honored place in twentieth-century literature. He has been compared to Proust and Joyce as an innovative stylist. His broad though somewhat indiscriminate erudition in contemporary philosophical trends prompted him to try to ground Symbolist theory in modern European thought and, along with Vyacheslav Ivanov, he was regarded as a major theoretician of Russian Symbolism.

In 1912 Bely espoused the anthroposophical teaching of the German social philosopher Rudolph Steiner. (Anthroposophy posits the existence of a spiritual world accessible to the higher human faculties.) Two years later, he settled in Dornach and participated in Steiner's project of erecting the Goetheanum there. Returning to Russia in 1916, he became one of the founding members of the Russian anthroposophist group. He enthusiastically greeted both the February and the Bolshevik Revolutions of 1917, interpreting them in an anthroposophical, mystical key, and was one of the few poets who became actively involved in the nascent Soviet culture. In 1921 he emigrated to Berlin but returned after two years to Soviet Russia, where he tried with limited success to adjust to the new cultural environment. These efforts left an indelible mark on the three volumes of his memoirs published in the Soviet Union in the 1930s. He died in Moscow in 1934.

## ■ ALEKSANDR BLOK

Indisputably the greatest poet of the Russian Symbolist movement, Aleksandr Blok belonged, like Andrey Bely, to the intellectual elite. Born in 1880, Blok grew up in the house of his grandfather, the Rector of Petersburg University. Bely and Blok knew each other's poetry long before they actually met and before they made their debuts in the press and started to correspond. This acquaintance came through their mutual friends—the family of Mikhail Soloviev, brother of the philosopher. (The Solovievs were Blok's distant relatives and the Bugaevs' neighbors in Moscow). To their contemporaries, Blok and Bely seemed loyal literary allies and closest friends, almost "twins." In reality, however, it was only during the short initial period between 1903 and 1905 that Bely and the Argonauts saw Blok's lyric as the expression of their aspirations.

In his 1956 autobiography Pasternak emphasized the kinship between the stylistic traits of Blok's poetry and the nature of the period of the 1905 Revolution:

> Adjectives without a noun, predicates without a subject, alarm, excitement, hide-and-seek, abruptness, whisking shadows—how well this style accorded with the spirit of the time, itself secretive, hermetic, underground, only just out of cellars and still using the language of conspiracy, the spirit of a time and of a tale in which the chief character was the city and the chief event was the street. [8]

The affinities of Symbolist poetic style with revolutionary reality were emphasized also in the first version of Bely's recollections of Blok:

> For both of us everything that was revealed in literature, whether verses or aspirations, originated in its own type of 'underground,' in which we,

**8** BORIS PASTERNAK. *An Essay in Autobiography*. Translated by Marya Harari. London, 1959. Translation has been slightly modified.

the conspirators for the future, exchanged verses as if they were political programs for some sort of future joint activity. But we were not able to crawl out of this underground. A mask deposited by the environment grew on both of us like an essential protective shield. (Might this be why so many masks figure in the poetry of A.A.[Blok]?) [9]

However, the "future joint activity" Bely had dreamed of proved to be impossible. Sharp differences in poetic style and aesthetic program became noticeable from the earliest stages of Blok's and Bely's literary careers. Their complex relationship was further complicated by Bely's tragic love affair with Blok's wife, Liubov Dmitrievna. By 1907 the once-united movement of the second-generation Symbolists split, and the former friends found themselves on opposite sides. Especially bitter was the quarrel that developed between the so-called mystical anarchists in Petersburg, supported by Vyacheslav Ivanov and Blok, on the one hand, and the "aesthetic Symbolists" who rallied around the monthly *Libra* edited by Valery Briusov in Moscow, on the other. [10] Bely was the principal contributor to the critical section of this journal, his attempts to establish a theoretical foundation for the movement marked by militant polemics.

Blok's position in this literary struggle dismayed his former friends among the Argonauts. In the literary battles between the *Libra* and a competing Moscow modernist periodical called *The Golden Fleece*, Blok sided with the latter and agreed to head its critical section. This period in Blok's work was dominated by openly political and social topics. "Populist" sentiments led him to praise the Realists, including Maxim Gorky, and harshly criticize the intellectual elite for its isolation from the people and its unwillingness to bridge this chasm. His lyrical drama *The Puppet Show*, written in January 1906, premiered in December of that year in Vera Komissarzhevskaya's theater in Petersburg. [11] The stage director

**9** ANDREY BELY.
*Vospominaniia ob Aleksandre Aleksandroviche Bloke* (Reminiscences of Aleksandr Blok). Letchworth, Hertfordshire, 1964.

**10** *Belye nochi* (White Nights). St. Petersburg, 1907.

This collection, devoted to the city of Petersburg, consists of poetry by authors particularly close to Blok at this time and was one of manifestations of the ties established between Blok and the Vyacheslav Ivanov circle. Mstislav Dobuzhinsky designed the cover.

**11** ALEKSANDR BLOK.
*Liricheskie dramy* (Lyrical Dramas). St. Petersburg, 1908.

"The lyric element," Blok observed in his preface, "is the most powerful in contemporary literature.... This is why, it seems, readers are sharply divided into two camps: those who escape the lyric and curse it, and those who are bewitched by it." In addition to Blok's "Balaganchik" (The Puppet Show), the collection included the plays "Korol na ploshchadi" (The King on the Square) and "Neznakomka" (Incognita) as well as Mikhail Kuzmin's incidental music for the productions. The cover illustration is by Konstantin Somov.

■ *Item number 11*

was Vsevolod Meyerhold, who also played the central role of Pierrot. This work shocked many of Blok's contemporaries because it both epitomized and parodied the main motifs of his own early lyric poetry. Perhaps Bely was most furious of all. He saw in *The Puppet Show* a sacrilegious jeer at the Solovievan utopia of the "Mysterium of Life," and a betrayal of the ideals of their common past.

The quarrel destroyed the original unity of the Symbolist school. Under attack by hostile anti-modernist forces since its emergence in the early 1890s, Symbolism now, for the first time in its history, faced a serious internal threat.

Besides Bely and Briusov, the *Libra* circle included two other former Argonauts—the poet and literary critic Ellis (L. Kobylinsky) and Sergey Soloviev. Sergey Mikhailovich Soloviev (1885-1942), close friend of Bely from school days and nephew of the philosopher Vladimir Soloviev, was a poet, translator, and philologist. Before the 1917 Revolution he published five original poetry collections including *Flowers and Incense* and *April.* [12, 13] His close personal and literary ties with Blok (his second cousin), were broken in 1905.

Though Sergey Soloviev was one of the most active participants of the Argonaut circle, his literary career was not particularly successful. His poetry reflected the artistic tendencies of the period, but lacked originality and imaginative vigor. In 1907 Blok deplored the "frightful banality" of his lyrics. Soloviev was one of the first among the Symbolists to revive poetic devices from the Pushkin epoch. The neo-classical tendencies in his poetry were influenced by Vyacheslav Ivanov's similar experiments, as he himself acknowledged.

In the literary battles of the time he aligned himself with Bely against the Petersburg Symbolists. This ideological and literary alliance was reinforced by close personal ties: Soloviev and his friends Ellis and Bely married three sisters. After the Revolution Soloviev published almost no original poems; only his translations appeared occasionally during the Soviet epoch. Unlike Bely and Blok, he vehemently rejected the Bolshevik Revolution. He became an Orthodox priest, but soon thereafter converted to Roman Catholicism. Under the Soviets, he was several times arrested and imprisoned in mental institutions.

Musagetes was the Moscow Symbolist publishing house (1910-17) founded by Émile Medtner, Bely, and Ellis in an attempt to resolve the severe crisis in Russian Symbolism by consolidating all Symbolist forces against the rising anti-Symbolist avant-garde groups. One of the earliest and most remarkable results of this attempt was Musagetes' publication in 1911 of Blok's fourth poetry collection, *The Night Hours.* [14]

In addition to its publishing activities, Musagetes organized seminars and workshops where novice poets could study Symbolist theory, metrical patterns in Russian verse, and new trends in European philosophy. Among these "Young Musagetes" were poets who later played decisive roles in Russian literature—Boris Pasternak, Marina Tsvetaeva, and Vladislav Khodasevich. This nurturing of a new generation of poets and the willingness to involve them in the literary ventures of Symbolism's leading figures is evident in the *Anthology* of 1911, which opened with a previously unpublished poem by Vladimir Soloviev. [15] Included, along with poems of Blok, Bely, Vyacheslav Ivanov, and Ellis, were works by the younger generation—Vladislav Khodasevich, Nikolay Gumilev, Maksimilian Voloshin, Mikhail Kuzmin—as well as such beginners as Tsvetaeva and Sergey Klychkov.

**12** SERGEY SOLOVIEV.
*Tsvety i ladan* (Flowers and Incense). Moscow, 1907.

**13** SERGEY SOLOVIEV.
*Aprel* (April). Moscow, 1910.

**14** ALEKSANDR BLOK.
*Nochnye chasy* (The Night Hours). Moscow, 1911.

**15** *Antologiia* (Anthology). Moscow, 1911.

## ■ IN IVANOV'S TOWER

During this period Vyacheslav Ivanov (1866-1949) emerged as a leading figure in the Symbolist movement and the most authoritative mentor of younger poets. Though the same age as the founders of the Decadent school, Ivanov made his poetic debut at about the same time as Blok and Bely, and his work was therefore regarded as belonging to second-generation Symbolism. His first book of poetry, *Lodestars*, appeared in 1903 after he met Briusov in Paris. [16] Ivanov's poetry was striking in its extensive use of archaic words borrowed from Old Church Slavonic and its references to Byzantine and Roman cultural traditions. These exotic stylistic features reflected Ivanov's early training abroad in classical philology and his great erudition. Not since before Pushkin had such sublime, solemn, and elevated style been seen in Russian poetry. Though Ivanov's experiments remained an isolated phenomenon, his attempts to rehabilitate archaic styles and genres, and his idea of using archaic language as a legitimate tool for the modernist liberation of poetry, encouraged other poets to go beyond the established boundaries of poetic language, and influenced even those poets who rebelled against the entire Symbolist culture—such as Velemir Khlebnikov.

Soon after the publication of *Lodestars*, Ivanov abandoned his plans for a scholarly career abroad and returned to Russia. He settled with his family in a spacious top-floor apartment of a house on Tavricheskaya Street in Petersburg. The Wednesday gatherings in the "Ivanov Tower," as his contemporaries called the apartment, became the single most important meeting place for the Petersburg intellectual elite and bohemian circles of the time. The meetings started in September 1905 and continued intermittently until the spring of 1912, when Ivanov moved to Moscow. All the prominent modernist literary figures, scholars, philosophers, artists, and even political figures visited the Tower, including the Merezhkovskys, Blok, Nikolay Berdiaev, Anatoly Lunacharsky, Konstantin Somov, Mstislav Dobuzhinsky, Theodore Zielinski, Bely, Kuzmin and Anna Akhmatova. The ambience prevailing at the Ivanov Wednesdays has often been described in the memoirs of the participants. [17] In his memoirs published in *Notes of the Dreamers*, V.A. Zorgenfrey characterized them as evenings of "verbal extravagance." Literature, philosophy, and politics were "interwoven in a complex game of sagacious musings, engendered by fertile erudition, and divinely inspired wit." [18]

**16** VYACHESLAV IVANOV. *Kormchie zvezdy* (Lodestars). St. Petersburg, 1903.

The poem "Krasota" (Beauty) was dedicated to Vladimir Soloviev. The idea for this verse book and its title were discussed by Ivanov with Soloviev shortly before the latter's death.

**17** VYACHESLAV IVANOV. *Cor ardens.* Moscow, 1911-12.

A two-volume collection of poetry written during the "Tower" years.

**18** V.A. ZORGENFREY. "Aleksandr Aleksandrovich Blok" in *Zapiski mechtatelei* (Notes of the Dreamers) 5(1922).

# THE CRISIS OF SYMBOLISM
## MIKHAIL KUZMIN AND THE ACMEISTS

In the preface to his poem *Retribution*, Aleksandr Blok recalled:

> The year 1910 brought the death of Komissarzhevskaya, the death of Vrubel, and the death of Tolstoy. The lyrical note died on the theatrical scene with Komissarzhevskaya; and with Vrubel there died the enormous personal world of the artists, the mad obstinacy, the insatiability of aspirations—to the point of lunacy. With Tolstoy died human tenderness, wise humanity.
>
> Further,...1910 meant the crisis of Symbolism....Trends rooted in hostility toward Symbolism and toward each other came into being that year: Acmeism, Ego-Futurism, and the first rudiments of Futurism. The slogan for the first of these trends was man, but already a different kind of man, entirely lacking in humanity-a kind of "primordial Adam."
>
> The winter of 1911 was filled with a courageous deep inner tension and trembling. I remember conversations at night where the consciousness of the inseparability and incompatibility of art, life, and politics first appeared. The thought, apparently aroused by strong jolts from without, simultaneously knocked on all of these doors, no longer content with the confluence of all that was easy and possible in the true mystic twilight of the years preceding the first Revolution and in the false mystic hangover that ensued as well. [19]

Said another participant, Elizaveta Kuzmina-Karavaeva, in her "Meetings with Blok," looking back as Mother Maria,

> This air of 1910 is simply indescribable....Everything was mixed together in this period: apathy, depression, decadence, and expectations of new catastrophes and changes. We lived in our enormous country as if on a desert island. Whereas Russia was illiterate, in our circle we...recited the Greeks by heart,...were enamored of the French Symbolists...knew the philosophy, theology, poetry and history of the entire world....This was another Rome in the age of decline....In a certain sense we were, of course, the revolution before the Revolution—so deeply, mercilessly and fatally were we digging the soil of the old tradition over again, so audaciously were we building bridges to the future. Yet at the same time this depth and audacity were combined with a perpetual decay....We were the last act in the tragedy of the rupture between the people and the intelligentsia. [20]

Such was the atmosphere in which Symbolist poetry faced its great crisis.

The decline of the Symbolist movement accelerated with the emergence of the literary forces united around a new Petersburg journal, *Apollo*. It first appeared in October 1909, coinciding with the discontinuation

**19** ALEKSANDR BLOK. *Vozmezdie* (Retribution). 1919.

**20** MOTHER MARIA (Elizaveta Kuzmina-Karavaeva). "Meetings with Blok" in *Sovremennye zapiski* (Contemporary Annals) 62(1936).

of *Libra* in Moscow. *Apollo*'s editorial board consisted of the young writers Sergey Makovsky, Nikolay Gumilev, Mikhail Kuzmin, Aleksey Tolstoy, and Sergey Auslender, who boldly questioned the Symbolist platform and stylistic principles. Vyacheslav Ivanov, Maksimilian Voloshin and Innokenty Annensky essentially determined the journal's editorial line. An interest in poetic technique replaced the metaphysical emphasis so characteristic of Symbolist aesthetics. The establishment of the "Academy of Verse," a group of poets who met at the *Apollo* editorial offices, reflected this change.

The pages of *Apollo* became the forum for a heated debate about the mission and literary destiny of Symbolism that laid bare the internal contradictions in Symbolist doctrine and showed the depth of the Symbolist crisis. The three most prominent Symbolists—Blok, Vyacheslav Ivanov, and Briusov—took part in the debate. Whereas Blok and Ivanov defended the theurgist notion of poetry and art, Briusov bluntly rejected it. He insisted that the Symbolist school had nothing to do with grandiose ambitions to transform life; on the contrary, its goals from the very start were confined to exploring technical aspects of poetic language and form. *Apollo*'s revisionist tendencies manifested themselves in Mikhail Kuzmin's call for "beautiful clarity" to counteract the intrinsic obscurity of Symbolist poetic style.

## ■ MIKHAIL KUZMIN

Mikhail Kuzmin (1872-1936) entered the literary scene in 1905 after studying musical composition with Rimsky-Korsakov in the 1890s and after extensive travels in Russia and abroad. His intellectual and artistic development was much influenced by his secondary-school friend Georgy Chicherin (1872-1936), who later became Minister for Foreign Affairs in the Soviet Government. Kuzmin's first poems were written merely as verbal texts for the songs he composed and performed at literary-artistic soirées. Originally, his reputation rested primarily on these pieces. His *Chime of Love*, issued by the Scorpio publishing house in 1910, contains a section of poems, followed by a corresponding section of musical scores. [21] The edition was illustrated by the drawings of two modernist artists, Sergey Sudeykin and Nikolay Feofilaktov. Kuzmin seemed to achieve the Symbolists' longed-for synthesis of verbal and musical perceptions, subordinating word to music, but without any metaphysical baggage.

Kuzmin's literary debut appealed to a wide audience and showed the freshness and originality of his themes and poetic style. The publication in 1906 of his novel *Wings*, in which he openly introduced homosexual themes into Russian literature, and the appearance of his first collection of poetry, *Nets*, placed him among the leading modernist authors. As early as 1907 Blok, in his article "On Drama," spoke of Kuzmin as "an artist through and through, a most subtle lyric poet, an ingenious dialectician in art." Blok added, "At the present moment, Kuzmin is the only writer of his kind. There has not been anyone like him in Russia before and I doubt whether there ever will be ...." [22] Kuzmin was a regular at the Ivanov Tower, becoming virtually a member of the Ivanov household after 1907.

The *Green Collection of Verse and Prose*, published by a group of young authors in December 1904, marked Kuzmin's first appearance as a writer. [23] This was evidently the only book produced by the publishing house of Shchelkanovo, which took its name from the family estate of the group's leader, Jury Verkhovsky (1873-1947). Two works by Kuzmin ap-

**21** MIKHAIL KUZMIN. *Kuranty liubvi* (Chime of Love). Moscow, 1910.

**22** ALEKSANDR BLOK. "O drame" (On Drama) in *Sobranie sochinenii* (Collected Works), Vol. 5. Moscow, 1962.

**23** *Zeleny sbornik stikhov i prozy* (The Green Collection of Verse and Prose). St. Petersburg, 1905.

pear in the *Green Collection*—a cycle of thirteen sonnets and a long dramatic poem, "The Story of the Knight d'Alessio," which was written as an opera libretto. Among the other contributors to the collection was Kuzmin's intimate friend Vyacheslav Menzhinsky (1874-1934), who was to gain prominence outside the literary field. After the Bolshevik Revolution he rose to high ranks in the GPU (the Soviet secret police) and was appointed its chief after the death of Feliks Dzerzhinsky. "The Novel of Demidov" in the *Green Collection* is Menzhinsky's only published work.

Kuzmin wrote in a variety of poetic genres, all characterized by hedonistic and frivolous themes and pastoral motifs, reminiscent of the traditions of *poésie fugitive* in French and Russian literature of the eighteenth and early nineteenth centuries. The perfection of his artistic expression was unique. Kuzmin was extraordinarily open-minded and consistently non-partisan on general questions of literary aesthetics. Even more extraordinary was the rapid evolution of his poetic style. In the mid-1910s Kuzmin was celebrated for his clear language. Just a few years later, this proponent of beautiful clarity created some of the most difficult, hermetic, and deliberately obscure poetry ever written in Russian. These dramatic changes in style, apparent in Kuzmin's collections *Parabolas* [24] and *The Trout Breaks the Ice*, coincided with the Revolution of 1917 and the Civil War period.

The lyrics of these turbulent times reveal unexpectedly close ties with the most radical trends in Russian modernist poetry, and Kuzmin's pamphlet *For the Two* is one of the earliest symptoms of this shift. [25] Its two poems show a striking affinity with the poetic styles of Mayakovsky and Khlebnikov. The poems were written in 1917 when Kuzmin was a neighbor of Mayakovsky and often met with him and with the Brik family. The second poem is dedicated to Lili Brik.

**24** MIKHAIL KUZMIN.
*Paraboly* (Parabolas). Berlin, 1923.
Gift of the Putnam Foundation

**25** MIKHAIL KUZMIN.
*Dvum* (For the Two). Petrograd, [1918]

■ *Item number 25*

*For the Two* was one of a dozen pamphlets issued in small editions by the publishing collective "Segodnia" (Today) in Petrograd during 1918-19. Although the primary goal of this short-lived enterprise was to produce children's books, it also advanced new principles of artistic design. The series included poetry and prose pieces by Aleksey Remizov, Evgeny Zamiatin, Sergey Esenin, and Sofia Dubnov-Erlich, whose verse booklet *Mother* was illustrated by Nina Liubavina. [26]

Dubnov-Erlich (b.1885) was the daughter of a famous Russian-Jewish historian and public figure, Shimon Dubnov (1860-1941), and the wife of a journalist, Henryk Erlich (1882-1941), later the leader of the Jewish Socialist party (Bund) in Poland. She worked on Gorky's journal *The Chronicle* (1915-17) and it was on Gorky's initiative that her poems were first published. In 1918, Dubnova and her family moved to Poland. After the outbreak of World War II, they fled from advancing Nazi troops to Soviet Russia where her husband was arrested, imprisoned, and later shot. She managed to come to the United States in 1942 with her two sons.

**26** SOFIA DUBNOV-ERLICH. *Mat* (Mother). Petrograd, [1918].

The mortal blow to the Symbolist school was dealt by the emergence in 1913 of two rebel factions—Acmeism and Futurism—which also opposed each other. Both groups bluntly rejected the philosophical premises of Symbolist doctrine (especially its theurgist ambitions), as well as many of its technical principles—notably, the indefiniteness of language. They both called for a return to earthly reality. But they differed sharply in their attitudes toward poetic language.

## ■ THE ACMEISTS

The origins of the Acmeist school go back to 1911 when two young poets, Sergey Gorodetsky (1884-1967) and Nikolay Gumilev (1886-1921), founded the "Guild of Poets." The term *Acmeism*, coined from the Greek word for "summit, peak, perfection, blossom," implied that the new group had absorbed the highest achievements of world culture. The alternative and less frequently used name—Adamism—stressed a contradictory aspect of its platform; namely, its freedom from the bondage of traditional cultural conventions. The close alliance between Gorodetsky and Gumilev stemmed not so much from artistic kinship as from their common literary ambitions and their desire to escape the Symbolist dogmas. [27] Whereas Gumilev's poetry by that time carried distinctly "foreign," exotic overtones, Gorodetsky, as one of his most famous verse collections, *Russia*, shows, was in search of a national poetic style. [28] His poetry was dominated by peasant motifs, by the revival of indigenous Slavic tribal traditions, by a neo-primitivism, and by the use of Slavic pagan mythology. [29] In this sense he foreshadowed the so-called peasant style in poetry, created in the mid-1910s by Kliuev, Esenin, and others. Together with them, Gorodetsky formed the short-lived literary association called "Beauty." His poem *To Pushkin* was published under the imprint of this association. [30]

In the Caucasus in 1916, Gorodetsky founded another "Guild of Poets," in which the radical avant-garde poets played a significant role. Upon his return to Petersburg in the summer of 1920 he shocked his old friends by his sudden political transformation. In the Soviet press he vehemently attacked his former associates and friends for their anti-Bolshevik stance. [31] The State Publishing House printed his *Sickle*, which sang paeans to Red Army commissars and proletarian poets. [32] This political metamorphosis marked a steep decline in his literary career.

**27** *Apollon* (Apollo), 1913:1.

The early manifestos of the Acmeist school - Gumilev's "Symbolism's Heritage and Acmeism" and Gorodetsky's "Some Currents in Contemporary Russian Literature" - first appeared in this literary journal.

**28** SERGEY GORODETSKY. *Rus* (Russia). Moscow, 1910.

**29** SERGEY GORODETSKY. *Iva* (Willow). St. Petersburg, 1913.

Gorodetsky's fifth book of poetry was published shortly before the first Acmeist manifestos. This copy is inscribed by the author to the noted literary critic Nikolay Karlovich Kulman (1871-1940).

**30** SERGEY GORODETSKY. *Pushkinu* (To Pushkin). Petrograd, 1915.

**31** SERGEY GORODETSKY. "Krasny Piter" (Red Petersburg). Typewritten manuscript with autograph corrections, 1920-23.

On loan from The Hoover Institution

Gorodetsky's long propaganda poem was written between 1920-1923. Only five excerpts from the first, shorter version of the poem were printed in the official Soviet newspaper *Izvestiia* in November 1920 and never again republished. Gorodetsky submitted it for publication to the Moscow publishing house "The Red Virgin Soil," but for unknown reasons it never appeared in its final form.

**32** SERGEY GORODETSKY. *Serp* (Sickle). Petersburg, 1921.

Never again did he regain the literary reputation he had enjoyed during the previous two decades. His artistic activity was gradually confined to compiling and translating opera librettos.

Important as Gorodetsky may have been in the earliest stages of the Acmeist movement, its real ideologue and leader was Gumilev. The Guild was made up of beginning poets, most of whom Gumilev had met while attending Romance philology courses at Petersburg University. The Guild meetings were devoted to discussions of the technical aspects of literary craft. Unlike the Symbolists, who saw poetry as the product of bursts of divine inspiration, they saw it as the result of methodical training and painstaking labor.

Only six of the Guild's members were considered "true Acmeists": Gumilev, Gorodetsky, Akhmatova, Mandelstam, Mikhail Zenkevich and Vladimir Narbut. The association of others with the Acmeist movement was rather loose and accidental. Yet despite the narrowness of its core circle, the Acmeist school exerted enormous influence on both Soviet and émigré poetry after the Revolution. Acmeists advanced the principle of clarity and exactness in place of the reticence, diffuseness, and vagueness of Symbolist language. They affirmed the world of real things in contrast to the elusive metaphysical abstractions that dominated Symbolist poetry.

Osip Mandelstam (1891-1938) was undoubtedly the best poet of the group. Though relatively inconspicuous during the early stages of the Acmeist movement and less prolific than its leaders, he eventually proved to be more influential and inspiring, both as poet and as theoretician, than anyone else in the group. Mandelstam's poetry first appeared in *Apollo* in 1910. His first full-length collection, *Stone*, followed thirteen years later. [33] More than anyone else he was also open to the newly

**33** OSIP MANDELSTAM. *Kamen* (Stone). Moscow, 1923.

This 1923 Moscow printing is the third edition.

■ *Item number 36*

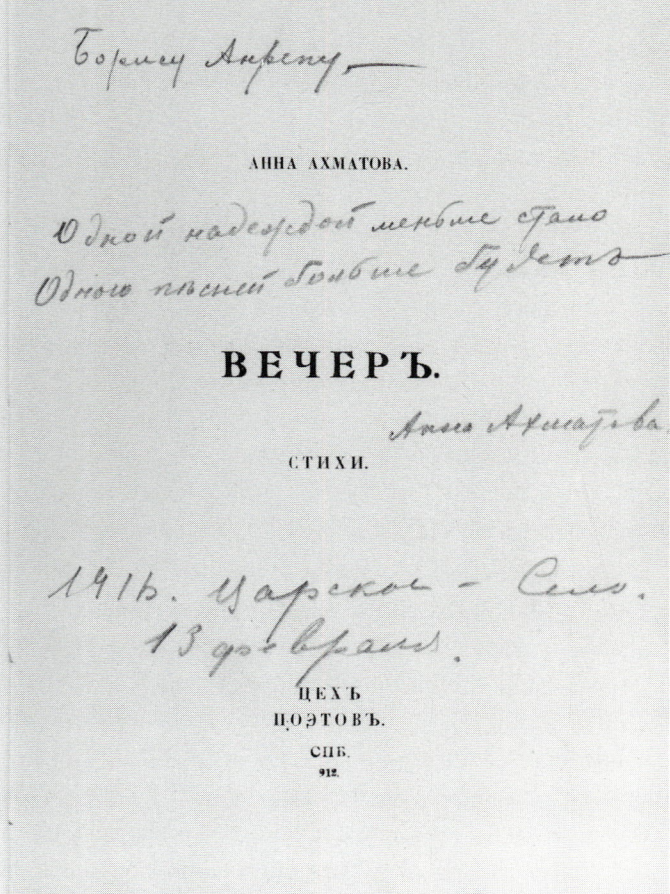

emerging trends that were to supplant Acmeism in the literary arena.

The group started its own publishing enterprise and in 1912 brought out a monthly of poetry and literary criticism, *Hyperboreus*, which ran for only ten issues. [34] Poems by Gorodetsky, Gumilev, Akhmatova, Mandelstam, Zenkevich, and Georgy Ivanov occupied the central place.

A number of individual volumes by the Acmeist poets were also published under the Hyperboreus imprint between 1912 and 1919. *Fourteen Poems* by Mikhail Zenkevich (1891-1973) was one of the last books issued by the house and perhaps the most distinctly "Acmeist" collection among Zenkevich's books. [35]

## ■ ANNA AKHMATOVA

One of the most significant and remarkable poetry collections produced by the Guild of Poets publishing house was *Evening* by Anna Akhmatova (1889-1966), which appeared, with a preface by Kuzmin, in March 1912. [36] The edition of only 300 copies brought suprisingly great success to its young author, who had just embarked on her professional literary career. Akhmatova started writing poems seriously soon after her marriage to Gumilev in 1910. During 1911 her lyrical poems were accepted for publication in several literary periodicals and miscellanies. *Evening* comprised the poems she had written since fall 1910, during Gumilev's trip abroad.

An even more sensational success greeted her next collection, *Rosary*, which was reissued nine times between 1914 and 1923. [37] With the exception of Igor Severyanin's work, hardly any other poetry of that time enjoyed such widespread popularity. It made Akhmatova one of the most popular poets of her age and certainly the best known among the Acmeists. Her love poems were read and recited throughout Russia. This unheard-of popular success, combined with broad critical appreciation, seems all the more striking in light of the decade of complete silence that befell her in Soviet Russia after 1924, when Akhmatova's intimate lyrics were judged incompatible with the new aesthetic values. Her famous *Requiem*, written during the Great Terror of the late 1930s, was not published in the Soviet Union until 1987. A new wave of Akhmatova's glory came during the 1940s, only to be interrupted by harsh attacks in the official press during the last years of Stalin's rule.

Some of Akhmatova's love poems were addressed to Boris Anrep (1883-1969), a prominent Russian artist who had lived mostly abroad since 1908. A number of his articles and notes on art were published in the Petersburg journal *Apollo*. He also wrote poetry. His poem "Man" was included—along with poems by Akhmatova, Gumilev, Vyacheslav Ivanov, Kuzmin, Mandelstam, Tsvetaeva and others—in the 1916 miscellany *Almanac of the Muses*. [38]

Called up for military duty, Anrep returned to Russia after the outbreak of World War I. It was during this stay in Russia that the love affair between him and Akhmatova began. In 1916 Anrep was dispatched to London to work with the Russian government delegation there. On his last visit to Russia, in autumn 1917, he and Akhmatova apparently did not meet. It was during this last visit, however, that she sent him an inscribed copy of her new verse collection *The White Flock*. [39] After the Bolshevik Revolution Anrep left Russia forever. He met Akhmatova only once therafter—in 1965 when she came to England to accept an honorary degree from Oxford University. The bulk of the love poems in *The White Flock* and *Plantain* (1921) are addressed to him.

---

**34** *Giperborei* (Hyperboreus) 9-10 (November-December 1913).

**35** MIKHAIL ZENKEVICH. *Chetyrnadtsat stikhotvorenii* (Fourteen Poems). Petrograd, 1918.

**36** ANNA AKHMATOVA. *Vecher* (Evening). St. Petersburg, 1912.

Inscribed by the author to Boris Anrep.

**37** ANNA AKHMATOVA. *Chetki* (Rosary). Petrograd, 1916.

Inscribed by the author to Anrep.

**38** *Almanakh Muz* (The Almanac of Muses). Petrograd, 1916.

Anrep inscribed this copy with a poem, dated February 13, 1916, which addresses his romantic involvement with Akhmatova.

**39** ANNA AKHMATOVA. *Belaia staia* (The White Flock). Petrograd, 1917

Inscribed by the author to Anrep.

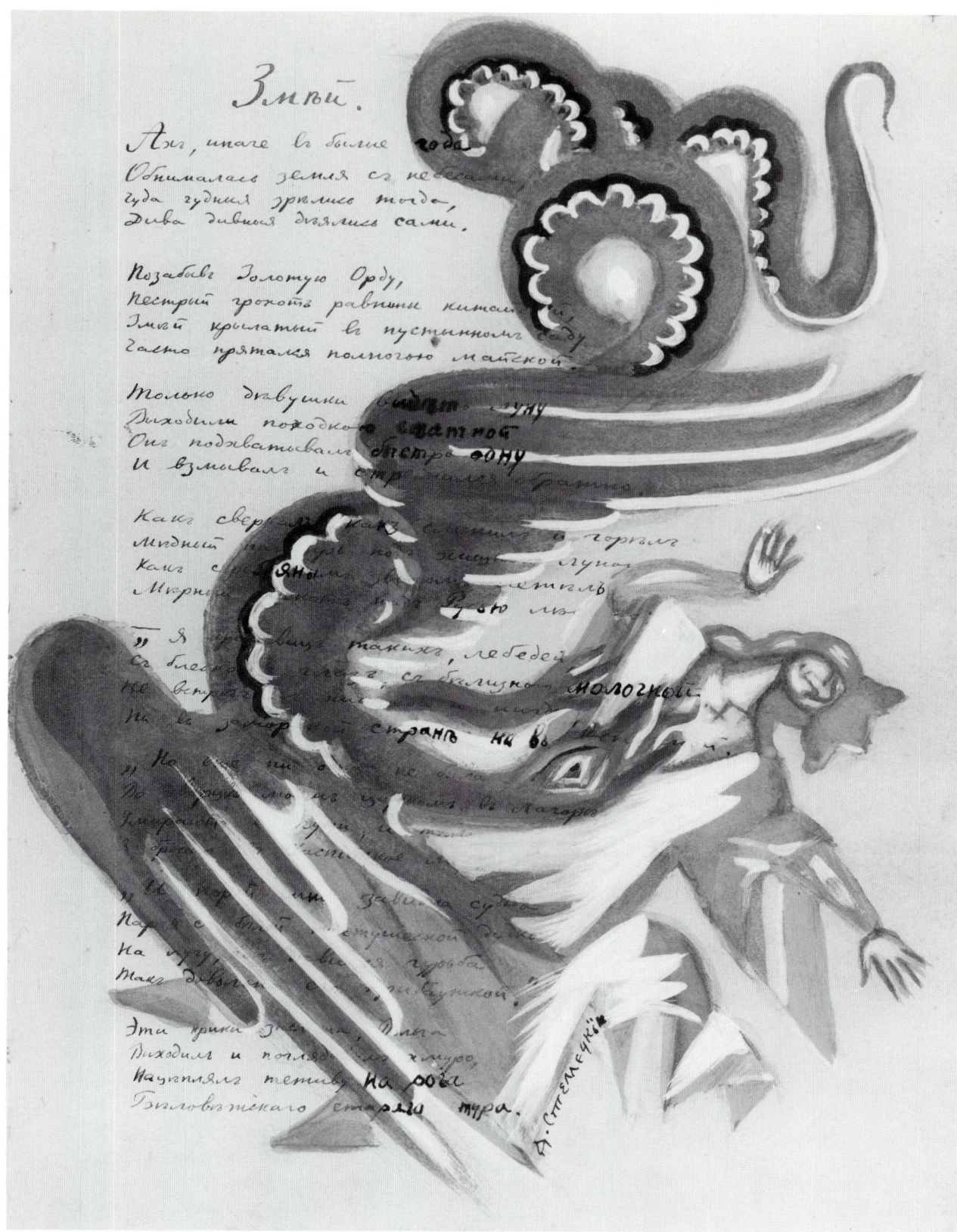

### ■ NIKOLAY GUMILEV

Another contributor to *Hyperboreus* was Nikolay Gumilev. His first genuinely "Acmeist" work and perhaps his best pre-Revolutionary poetry collection, *The Quiver*, appeared in 1916. [40, 41]

Soon after the outbreak of World War I Gumilev joined the army as a volunteer. His military career is reflected in his official record, shown here. [42] Gumilev was twice awarded the highest Russian combat decoration for bravery—the St. George Cross. In spring 1917 he was ordered to the Allied Army on the Thessalonica Front. Unable, however, to reach his Greek destination, he stayed in Paris from July 1917 onward, at the

■ *Item number 45*

**40** NIKOLAY GUMILEV.
*Kolchan* (The Quiver). Moscow, 1916.

**41** NIKOLAY GUMILEV.
"Sentimentalnoe stikhotvorenie dlia T.M. Devel" (Sentimental Poem for T.M. Devel). Autograph manuscript, January 15-25, 1905.

On loan from The Hoover Institution

**42** "Posluzhnoi spisok." Gumilev's military dossier. Typewritten document, 1916.

On loan from The Hoover Institution

■ *Item number 46*

disposal of the Russian Government's military representative. [43, 44] Among his close friends there were two members of the Russian colony in Paris, artists Nathalie Goncharova and Mikhail Larionov. Gumilev's handwritten album of poems is a testimony to their friendship. [45, 46]

In January Gumilev was sent to England. He returned to Petersburg in April of 1918, after the Bolshevik government had signed the fateful peace treaty with Germany.

**43** "Raport." Gumilev's request to be sent to the Persian front. Autograph document signed, January 8, 1918.

On loan from The Hoover Institution

**44** NIKOLAY GUMILEV. "Memoire concernant une possibilité éventuelle d'un recrutement...." Autograph manuscript signed. ca.1918.

On loan from The Hoover Institution

**45** NIKOLAY GUMILEV. "Stikhi" (Poems). Autograph manuscript. ca.1917.

On loan from The Hoover Institution

The manuscript, illustrated by Nathalie Goncharova and Dmitry Stelletsky, eventually became the possession of Gleb Struve, noted scholar of twentieth-century Russian literature.

**46** MIKHAIL LARIONOV. Portraits of Gumilev. Two original pencil drawings.

On loan from The Hoover Institution

# REVOLT IN POETRY: FUTURISM

Futurism took a more militant stance and had a much more profound impact on the literary scene than did the early Acmeist publications. At one point Gumilev entertained the idea of joining ranks with the Futurists against Symbolism. Some common principles and slogans—notably, rejection of the vagueness and metaphysical orientation of language in the Symbolist lyric, and keen interest in the early stage of Russian and Slavic life—made such an alliance seem plausible. Yet all attempts to form a broad anti-Symbolist coalition ran aground because of the Futurists' insolent attacks against their potential allies. From the start, the Futurist poets aligned themselves with the most extreme camps in avant-garde painting and theater, rebelling against all established cultural values, past or present, and scandalizing the public with their behavior. The carrot Mayakovsky wore in his lapel instead of a carnation is a small example. The emergence of Futurism also polarized the literary scene, and caused feverish regroupings.

## ■ EGO-FUTURISM

Russian Futurism was even divided against itself, from the first stage onward. One faction was formed in fall 1911 by Igor Severyanin (Igor Lotaryov, 1887-1941). This group called itself Ego-Futurism, adding "Ego" to the term used since 1908 by Filippo Marinetti's followers among the Italian avant-garde poets and artists. [47] The prefix expressed the extreme individualism advocated by the group. Along with the name, Severyanin and his cohort adopted the shocking literary behavior—the self-advertisement, pretentiousness, and self-glorification—of their Western counterparts. Severyanin's aesthetics were distinctly intuitivist. His poetry was marked by mannered or foreign neologisms and individualistic themes. Severyanin soon broke with the group he himself had created. The vicissitudes of his Futurist period were described in his autobiographical verse-novel, *Bells of the Cathedral of Feelings*, written in exile in 1923. [48]

After Severyanin's departure, Ivan Ignatyev (the penname of Ivan Kazansky) took over as the leader of the Ego-Futurist movement. His group and publishing enterprise were called the "Petersburg Herald." Between

**47** IGOR SEVERYANIN.
*Mirreliya: Novye poezy* (Mirrelia: New Poesas). Berlin, 1922.

The poem "Poeza istiny" (Poesa of Truth), although written in 1912, was not published until 1922 because of censorship. In it Severyanin defines his poetic philosophy and provides his reasons for adding the prefix *ego-* to the word futurism. The neologism *poesa*, coined by Severyanin and widely used by his followers, was designed to replace the traditional term *poem*. *Mirrelia* refers to the imaginary "Land of Mirra" named after the Russian woman poet Mirra Lokhvitskaya, who was much admired by Severyanin.

**48** IGOR SEVERYANIN.
*Kolokola sobora chuvstv* (Bells of the Cathedral of Feelings). Tartu, 1925.

■ *Item number 47*

1912 and early 1914 the "Herald" brought out a number of individual collections and nine miscellanies reflecting the group's shifting aesthetic positions and the dynamics of its literary alliances. The active history of the Ego-Futurist group ended with the suicide of its leader. Ignatyev, then thirty-one, killed himself January 20, 1914, after trying unsuccessfully to kill his wife with a razor the day after their wedding. His first and only poetry collection, *The Scaffold of Ego-Futurism*, opened with a poem that took on tragic and prophetic meaning in light of his death. [49]

One of the most typical representatives of the Ego-Futurist movement was Konstantin Olimpov (1880-1940). The poems in his pamphlet-size collection *Nerves, the Jugglers* develop the eccentric themes and imagery so prevalent in the works of this generation of poets. [50] On the opening page, Olimpov published a poem addressed to him by his father, the famous Russian pre-Symbolist poet Konstantin Fofanov (1862-1911). This poem illuminates both the collection's title, and the author's choice of the penname Olimpov (derived from the Greek Mt. Olympus).

Olimpov's own opening poem starts with the line "Ia khochu byt dushevno bolnym" (I want to be insane). This wish soon came true, as the testimony of his contemporaries leaves no doubt. On one occasion, he stood in the Marsovo Pole Square in Petrograd and offered passersby tickets to fly to the Moon. Olimpov's last publication appeared in 1922, when he was already almost completely forgotten by his contemporaries, and only "Oberiu," a group of young Leningrad poets—outcasts like himself—still maintained contact with this relic of the Ego-Futurist era.

**49** IVAN IGNATYEV.
*Eshafot ego-futury* (The Scaffold of Ego-Futurism). 1914.

**50** KONSTANTIN OLIMPOV.
*Zhonglery-nervy* (Nerves, the Jugglers). St. Petersburg, 1912.

*Item number 50*

After the death of Ignatyev, Severyanin and some of his pupils made sporadic attempts to revive Ego-Futurist aesthetic values and poetics, if not the movement itself, by publishing several joint miscellanies. Severyanin, one of the most prolific and popular poets of the period, was proclaimed "King of Russian Poetry" in 1918, thus outdoing his rivals, Vladimir Mayakovsky and Konstantin Balmont. Severyanin emigrated to Estonia in 1919, where he published his *Estonian Poesas*. [51] He remained there until his death in 1941, several months after the German invasion. Inside Soviet Russia, the traditions of Ego-Futurism disappeared without a trace. However, the books of Severyanin's disciples, such as Sergey Alymov's *The Kiosk of Tenderness* [52], and Aleksey Masainov's *Departing Ships* [53] and *The Beast's Face* [54], were published after the Revolution in such widely separated centers as Harbin and Paris, testifying to the vitality of the Ego-Futurist style abroad.

## ■ CUBO-FUTURISM

Ego-Futurism introduced the term *futurism* into Russian culture, but it was the Cubo-Futurist wing of the avant-garde that really transformed Russian poetry. Embodying the rebellious spirit that was increasingly felt in Russian culture of the period, it took to extremes all the artistic direc-

**51** IGOR SEVERYANIN.
*Pühajõgi: Estliandskie poezy* (Pühajõgi: Estonian Poesas). Tartu, 1919.

**52** SERGEY ALYMOV.
*Kiosk nezhnosti* (The Kiosk of Tenderness). Harbin, 1920.

**53** ALEKSEY MASAINOV.
*Otkhodiashchie korabli* (Departing Ships). Paris, 1925.

Included in this work are poems which first appeared in two miscellanies Masainov coauthored with Igor Severyanin in 1916-1917. At the end of the Civil War Masainov fled Russia and eventually settled in Hollywood.

**54** ALEKSEY MASAINOV.
*Lik zveria* (The Beast's Face). Paris, 1924.

tions explored by the previous modernist movements. It shocked contemporaries by its uncompromising hostility toward the cultural past and by its open disdain for its literary rivals.

Among the group's members were two of the greatest Russian poets of our century—Vladimir Mayakovsky (1893-1930) and Velemir Khlebnikov (1885-1922). Although these two giants must be given their due, other Cubo-Futurists, such as David Burliuk and Aleksey Kruchenykh, also exerted tremendous influence.

The Cubo-Futurists came to accept this name only in 1913, well after some of their sensational early appearances. Militantly anti-Western, and eager to dissociate themselves from the Italian Futurists, they called themselves *budetliane*, a term coined by Khlebnikov from the Russian root meaning "future." When Marinetti came to Russia in early 1914, they boycotted or interrupted his readings.

The term Cubo-Futurism, which eventually won out, reflected these poets' intimate ties with avant-garde painting. Almost all the *budetliane* had trained as painters at some point in their careers, and they contributed to the exhibitions, miscellanies, and public discussions organized by such avant-garde groups as the Union of Youth, Donkey's Tail, and Jack of Diamonds. Their artistic backgrounds and their fascination with the works of Picasso, Braque, Malevich, and Tatlin are clearly felt in their notion of the "self-oriented word" (devoid of references), their violation of grammatical rules, their use of truncated, mutilated words, and most of all in their inauguration of *zaum* (another of Khlebnikov's coinages; literally, "beyond mind"; picked up by the Futurists for a kind of poetry or poetic language usually described in translation as "transrational" or nonsense poetry, often using words constructed on Slavic roots).

This new attitude toward art and language resulted in closer collaboration between writers and painters, in the production of "artists' books." Among the artists involved were the most prominent figures of the Russian avant-garde—Mikhail Larionov, Nathalie Goncharova, Vladimir Tatlin, Pavel Filonov, Olga Rozanova, and Kazimir Malevich. These collaborations led to dramatic changes in the graphic design and visual language used in the book arts.

The Futurists' idea of "liberated words" and their rejection of all established values found expression even in the external features of their publications—in the deliberate use of crude papers and unattractive wrapping materials, and in the mixing of various typefaces on a single page and even within a single word. Some of their works were published as mimeographed booklets in which the artist's illustrations and the author's handwriting interact to heighten the shocking effect of the verbal content. This new approach can be seen in the published version of Khlebnikov and Kruchenykh's poem *A Game in Hell*. [55] This mimeographed book came out late in 1913, with drawings by Rozanova and Malevich. Such Futurist editions did away with the traditional view of illustration as an extraneous adornment or a luxury.

The third—and last—issue of the periodical *The Union of Youth* (1913) was another example of close cooperation between poet and artist. [56] This issue marked the formal alliance of the art group led by Filonov and Rozanova with the *budetliane*. Among its contributors were Khlebnikov, Burliuk, and Kruchenykh.

The first edition of *The Croaked Moon*, published early in 1913, was significant because it was here that the group first called itself Futurists. Moreover the opening article by Benedikt Livshits (1886-1939), "The

**55** VELEMIR KHLEBNIKOV AND ALEKSEY KRUCHENYKH. *Igra v ady* (A Game in Hell). St. Petersburg, 1914.

**56** *Soiuz molodezhi* (The Union of Youth). 3(1913).

Liberation of the Word," is one of the most important theoretical statements of the Futurist movement. The central place in the collection was given to Mayakovsky's and Khlebnikov's works (including the latter's famous "Liubkho," consisting exclusively of words coined from the Russian root denoting "love").

No less important was the second edition of the miscellany, which appeared in spring 1914 during the heydey of Russian Futurism. [57] It reflected the changes that had occurred in the literary scene during the intervening year. For this edition, the Cubo-Futurists were joined by two members of the Ego-Futurist "Mezzanine of Poetry" just established in Moscow, Vadim Shershenevich and Konstantin Bolshakov. The two new participants were given prominent places in the book: Shershenevich's cycle of poems (dedicated to Bolshakov) opened the poetry section, whereas Bolshakov's verses closed it.

### ■ A FUTURIST ALLIANCE

The alliance between the Cubo-Futurists and the Mezzanine of Poetry became an important factor in Russian literary life: for the first time the animosity between modernist factions gave way to a Futurist coalition in poetry. The coalition became possible primarily because of basic similarities in poetic content and style among three younger poets—Mayakovsky, Shershenevich and Bolshakov. The three of them shared not only themes (predominantly urban), but also expressive means and poetic language: the turn toward accentual verse and new kinds of rhyme, highly metaphorical style, and extensive use of neologisms distinct from *zaum*. The special significance of the second edition of the *The Croaked Moon* lies in the fact that it documents the short-lived alliance between Mayakovsky and Shershenevich. Very soon thereafter, by the summer of 1914, in fact, the ties were broken, never to be restored. Shershenevich was unable to find other allies and to organize another literary group until after the October Revolution.

■ *Item number 55*

**57** *Dokhlaia luna* (The Croaked Moon). Moscow, 1914.

Gift of Richard Cydzik

The work includes an illustration by David Burliuk's younger brother, Vladimir Burliuk (1886-1917).

Vadim Shershenevich (1893-1942), son of a law professor at the Kazan and Moscow universities, was the most pro-Western of the Russian Futurists. The only one to acknowledge Marinetti's influence, he translated two of the Italian's prose works and in 1914 published a Russian translation of the literary manifestos of Italian Futurism. Shershenevich's collection *Automobile Gait* contains his major poems from the Futurist period. [58]

Shershenevich's closest associate in the Mezzanine of Poetry was Konstantin Bolshakov (1895-1940), a young poet whose lyrics were highly praised by Mayakovsky and Pasternak. With Shershenevich, as already noted, Bolshakov entered the Cubo-Futurist group of Mayakovsky and Burliuk. Later he joined yet another Futurist faction, the Centrifuge Futurist publishing enterprise organized by Sergey Bobrov, Nikolay Aseev and Boris Pasternak. The most comprehensive collection of Bolshakov's poetry, *The Sun at the End of Its Flight*, illustrated by El Lissitzky and published in spring of 1916, is the monument of that involvement. [59] This was also Bolshakov's last published book of poetry. After the Revolution he switched to prose, and his 1920s novels eclipsed his poems in the public memory.

Another member of the Mezzanine of Poetry, Sergey Tretyakov (1892-1939), achieved wide recognition only after the October Revolution. His first collection of poems, *The Iron Pause*, containing mostly his early Ego-Futurist work, was published in Vladivostok in 1919. [60] During the Civil War Tretyakov lived in the eastern region of Russia, serving for some time as Deputy Minister of Education in the government of the Far Eastern Republic. In Chita, capital of this short-lived state, between 1921 and 1922 there arose the Futurist group "Creativity," in which Tretyakov and Nikolay Aseev were the most active participants. Upon his return to Russia in 1922, Tretyakov became a leading member of the Left Front of the Arts (LEF) founded by Mayakovsky, and remained loyal to its principles even when Mayakovsky broke with the group. One of the most prominent figures in the international movement of revolutionary writers in the 1920s and '30s, Tretyakov was arrested, charged with espionage for Japan, and killed during Stalin's "great terror" years.

## ■ LIREN

Nikolay Aseev (1889-1963) entered the Futurist camp in spring 1914 when the Moscow group Centrifuge published its first miscellany. He and his co-founders Sergey Bobrov and Boris Pasternak strove to find their own path among Futurist groups. The distinguishing trait of the Centrifuge was its rejection of the nihilistic approach to cultural traditions and of the intentionally shocking self-advertisement so characteristic of Cubo-Futurist poetry. However, Aseev's commitment to the Centrifuge was always weaker than that of Bobrov and Pasternak, and later in 1914 he established his own Futurist publishing enterprise in Kharkov. Liren, as it was called, became a formidable competitor of the Centrifuge. One of Liren's books was Aseev's enigmatically titled collection *Oi konin dan okein*. [61] He claimed that the title meant "I love your eyes" in the gypsy language. However, the cover of the book, decorated as it is with the words "Allah is merciful" in Arabic script, points toward a different cultural tradition. Velemir Khlebnikov, an influential mentor of Aseev in poetry, once spoke of his "Persian, Hafiz-like rapture over verbal foliage in all the purity of its bloom."

Aseev spent the Civil War years in the Russian Far East. Returning to Moscow in January 1922, he soon became one of Mayakovsky's closest allies, always ready to lend his full support, and to echo the most radical

**58** VADIM SHERSHENEVICH. *Avtomobilya postup* (Automobile Gait). Moscow, 1916.

**59** KONSTANTIN BOLSHAKOV. *Solntse na izlete* (The Sun at the End of its Flight). Moscow, 1916.

**60** SERGEY TRETYAKOV. *Zheleznaia pauza* (The Iron Pause). Vladivostok, 1919.

This copy is signed by its former owner, Petr Neznamov (Petr Lezhankin, 1889-1941), a minor futurist poet. Together with Tretyakov and Aseev he participated in the Far East literary group "Tvorchestvo" (Creativity) in the city of Chita. At the end of the Civil War Neznamov returned to Moscow and joined the editorial board of Mayakovsky's journal *Lef*.

**61** NIKOLAY ASEEV. *Chetvertaia kn. stikhov. "Oi konin dan okein"* (The Fourth Book of Poems: "Oi konin dan okein"). Moscow, 1916.

LEF slogans. This slavish devotion to LEF doctrine led to a palpable decline in his poetic creativity. The first decade of his literary career was undoubtedly the most fruitful. The freshness and stylistic independence of his early lyrics were praised by the best poets of the generation—Mayakovsky, Khlebnikov, and Pasternak. His *Selected Poems* [62] collects the verse written during those formative years, whereas his *Steel Nightingale* [63] reflects the transition to the new aesthetic principles promulgated by Mayakovsky's group under the Soviets. One of the *Steel Nightingale* poems is noteworthy as a poetic response to Pasternak's *My Sister, Life*, which Aseev very much admired.

Despite the difficulties of war-time communication, Liren's publishing activities continued, even while Aseev was in the eastern region. It published very little, however, beyond the works of Grigory Petnikov (1894-1971), Aseev's partner in Liren, and a minor but interesting Futurist poet and translator of German Romantics and Expressionists. [64] Like Aseev, Petnikov was an ardent follower of Velemir Khlebnikov. The miscellany *Liren*, the last joint project of this group, was released in Moscow in 1920, while book production was all but frozen. [65] Although slender in size, this pamphlet had great historical weight: besides Petnikov himself and Elena Guro (1877-1913; posthumously published) it brought together the greatest poets of the Futurist generation—Mayakovsky, Khlebnikov, Pasternak, and Aseev. Of particular significance was Khlebnikov's article "Our Fundamentals," perhaps his most important theoretical statement to appear after the Revolution. It addresses two central issues that preoccupied him—his linguistic theory and his idea of the regular recurrence or periodicity of great historical events and world cataclysms, an idea that would allow one to forecast the future.

The anthology *Moscow Masters*, published in spring 1916, was another attempt to unite the various factions of the Futurist movement. [66] It also aimed to prove that the movement was abandoning its rebellious and extremist tendencies, and becoming much more "civilized." No other Futurist book was so elegantly printed. Besides literary works by Khlebnikov, Benedikt Livshits, Burliuk, Bolshakov and others, color reproductions of paintings by Burliuk, Petr Konchalovsky, Aristarkh Lentulov, and Martiros Sarian appeared in the volume.

## ■ MINOR FUTURISTS

Dmitry Petrovsky (1892-1955), whose work was influenced by both Khlebnikov and Pasternak, stood out among the minor Futurists in that he was directly involved in the Revolution. In the Civil War he fought with the Red guerillas in the Ukraine. During that time he published his first and perhaps best poetry book, *The Deserted Autumn*, in Gorodnia, with the short-lived and whimsically named Baby Camel Publishing House. [67] His intriguing recollections of his meetings with Khlebnikov were published in the first issue of Mayakovsky's magazine *Lef* (1923). But soon thereafter Petrovsky broke with LEF and stayed isolated in the literary scene, rejecting the LEF doctrine as a betrayal of the original Futurist principles.

The Futurist poetic revolution spawned a host of diverse and ephemeral literary phenomena, groups of writers following the new artistic principles to various degrees, and inhabiting the periphery of the avantgarde. Though their artistic accomplishments may seem negligible, the works of these writers throw into relief the work of the leading avantgarde figures. The anthology *Championship of Poets*, published in Petersburg in 1913, was one of the earliest responses of "mass culture" to the tri-

**62** NIKOLAY ASEEV.
*Izbran* (Selected Poems). Moscow, 1923.

**63** NIKOLAY ASEEV.
*Stalnoi solovei* (The Steel Nightingale). Moscow, 1922.

**64** GRIGORY PETNIKOV.
*Porosl solntsa* (Shoots of the Sun). Petersburg, 1922.

**65** *Liren*. Moscow, 1920.

**66** *Moskovskie mastera* (Moscow Masters). Moscow, 1916.

On loan from The Hoover Institution

**67** DIMITRY PETROVSKY.
*Pustynnaia osen* (The Deserted Autumn). Gorodnia, 1920.

umph of Futurism. [68] None of the contributors to the volume has left any trace in literature except for Ivan Evdokimov, whose poems open the book, and who later became a well-known Soviet prose writer. Shown is a copy of the anthology that bears the signature and marginal comments of its former owner, Aleksey Tikhomirov, dated November 1913. Tikhomirov's title-page annotation provides information about one contributor otherwise unknown to literary scholars—his university friend, the poet Anatoly Puchkov. According to Tikhomirov, after the October Revolution Puchkov was appointed People's Commissar for Food Supply in the Petrograd area (the so-called Northern Commune). He left no mark on Russian literature after the late 1920s.

### ■ DAVID BURLIUK

David Burliuk (1882-1967) called himself the Father of Russian Futurism, and many agreed with this title. His boundless energy and his revolutionary instinct in art had made him the leader of the *budetliane*, and until 1918 he participated in almost all the group's collective publishing projects. His last joint ventures with Mayakovsky and Vasily Kamensky were reading in the Poets' Café, publishing the only issue of the *Newspaper of the Futurists* (March 1918), and acting in the silent film *Not for Money Born*.

The performances in the Poets' Café became more sporadic and less scandalous when, in April 1918, Burliuk left Moscow and started across Siberia for the Far East. Upon arriving at a town on his way, Burliuk usually arranged an exhibition of the Futurist paintings he carried with him. After the showing he would talk about the accomplishments of the new art and recite Mayakovsky's, Khlebnikov's, and Kamensky's poems as well as his own. In the Far East, just as in Moscow, he became a driving force behind Futurist literary activities. Between 1920 and 1922 he lived in Japan, where he established ties with the local avant-garde artists. His 1921 article "The Japanese Futurists" describes his meetings with them. [69] The manuscript of the article, shown here, was sent to Aleksandr Aleksandrovich Gzel. An acquaintance of Burliuk's in Vladivostok, Gzel later moved to Harbin (Manchuria), where he ran a small publishing house and edited the periodical *Vial*. Burliuk later described his overall impressions of the Japanese period in his pamphlet *Across the Pacific*. [70]

In the fall of 1922 Burliuk moved to the United States, settling in New York. After his exodus his role in Russian letters gradually diminished, despite his ebullient disposition and tireless activity. His attempts in the mid-1920s to organize a group of "proletarian" writers failed, and only a few collections were published. Even Mayakovsky's visit to the United States in 1925 could not help Burliuk revive Futurism in a new social and cultural environment. Burliuk's numerous publishing projects, including the series *Color and Rhyme*, were largely confined to self-advertisement and backward looks at the early history of Russian Futurism. In his new country he was known as an artist, not as a poet.

### ■ VLADIMIR MAYAKOVSKY

Pasternak once defined Mayakovsky's historical mission as justifying the Futurist movement and that entire generation. Those who knew the young Mayakovsky were struck by his immense, overwhelming inner strength. He seemed to embody the very essence of artistic genius, its hypnotic, irresistible power. Futurism as a movement might claim important artistic achievements, and Khlebnikov, Burliuk, and Kruchenykh might shock the public with their innovations, but it was Mayakovsky who gave deep and ultimately tragic expression to the rebellious spirit of

**68** *Chempionat poetov* (Championship of Poets). St. Petersburg, 1913.

**69** DAVID BURLIUK. "Iaponskie Futuristy" (The Japanese Futurists). Autograph manuscript.

On loan from The Hoover Institution

**70** DAVID BURLIUK. *Po Tihomu okeanu* (Across the Pacific). New York, 1927.

Burliuk inscribed this copy to Georgy Grebenshchikov (1883-1964), a noted Russian émigré prose writer.

the new movement and to revolutionary culture in general. It was not by chance that his first large work, *Vladimir Mayakovsky*, was a tragedy in which the distinction between author and hero was blurred. In performance the poet himself played the central role.

Korney Chukovsky, who knew Mayakovsky by 1913, wrote in his memoirs:

> One could already see in him a man of a grand fate, a grand historical mission. Not that he was haughty. But he walked among people as if he were Gulliver, and although he did not in the least seek to make them feel like Lilliputians next to him, it somehow happened that even the most conceited and arrogant people could not look down upon him.

As a teenager, Mayakovsky joined the Bolshevik party, carried out some underground assignments, and was arrested three times. Though he soon withdrew from politics and never renewed his formal party membership, the spirit of rebellion permeated his artistic life. He was a student at the Moscow School for Painting, Sculpture and Architecture when it was the epicenter of avant-garde ferment in Russia. Like many of those later known as Futurists, he was preparing himself for a professional artistic career, contributing to the modernist exhibitions and heated public debates.

It was here that Mayakovsky met and became friends with Burliuk. In the fall of 1912, he showed Burliuk his first lyrical poems. "I think of David with my usual love," Mayakovsky later wrote. "He is an excellent friend and my true teacher. Burliuk has made me a poet." Burliuk's wildly enthusiastic response to the poems led Mayakovsky to join Burliuk's group of young *budetliane* poets, and Mayakovsky soon emerged as a leader of the movement. With Burliuk, Khlebnikov, and Kruchenykh, he wrote a famous manifesto which called for throwing the Russian classics overboard from the steamship of modernity. Published in the collection *A Slap in the Face of Public Taste* in December 1912, it marked the begin-

■ *Item number 71*

ning of wide and sometimes scandalous fame for Mayakovsky and his group, which soon adopted the name Cubo-Futurists.

Mayakovsky's best work—his long poem *A Cloud in Trousers*—had a profound effect on Russian poetry. [71] It was a genuine revolution in virtually all aspects of lyrical expression—in thematics, rhythmical structure, vocabulary, poetic syntax and authorial voice. The completion of the work in July of 1915 coincided with Mayakovsky's meeting Lili and Osip Brik, who were to become his closest friends. Lili Brik (1891-1978) became more than a friend. She was the great love of Mayakovsky's life. Said Viktor Shklovsky in *Mayakovsky and His Circle*, "And so he fell in love with her at first sight, and, actually, forever—till the very loss of weight." When Mayakovsky had trouble finding a publisher for *Cloud in Trousers*, Osip Brik subsidized its printing, and the poem appeared as a separate book in September 1915. The three friends maintained a ménage à trois for many years.

Several sections of the *Cloud* were so heavily censored that on some pages every verse line was replaced by dots. Lili Brik recalled "how Khlebnikov [had] listened to the 'Cloud' with bated breath hundreds of times, and when he received the book, he began to inscribe into his copy the passages which had been censored."

*Man* was the last of four long poems written by Mayakovsky in the pre-Soviet period. [72] Subtitled *Thing*, it challenged all traditional definitions of literary genres and pointed to an essential element in avant-garde aesthetic doctrine—the elimination of boundaries between real life

**71** VLADIMIR MAYAKOVSKY. *Oblako v shtanakh* (A Cloud in Trousers). Petrograd, 1915.

The copy shown belonged to Rudolph Abich (1901-1940), a friend of Khlebnikov. Abich's annotations fill in many of the lines and sections which had been censored from Mayakovsky's work.

**72** VLADIMIR MAYAKOVSKY. *Chelovek* (Man). Moscow, 1918.

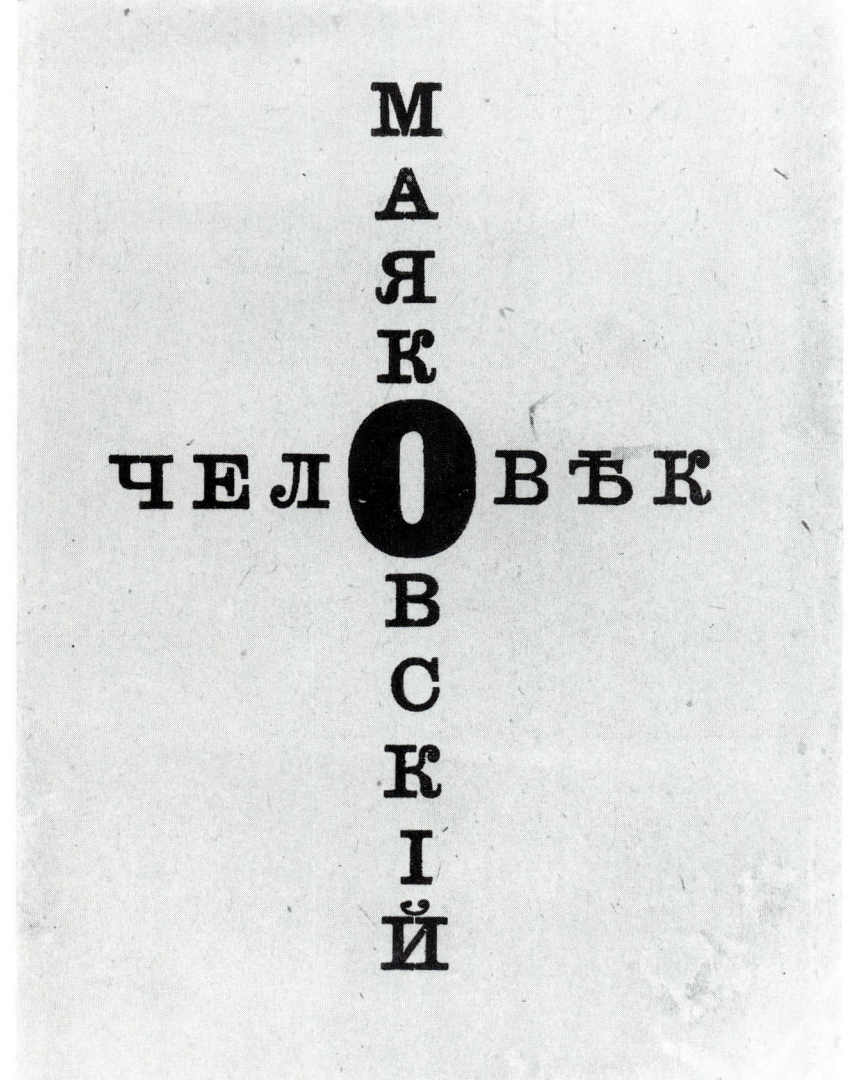

■ *Item number 72*

and artistic text. Completed in 1917, the poem appeared simultaneously with the second, uncensored edition of *A Cloud in Trousers*, in February 1918, under the imprint of the "ASIS" (Association of Socialist Art). This was a climactic moment in the poet's literary career. Never again would Mayakovsky regain the lyrical intensity and power of his pre-Revolutionary work.

It came as no surprise that Mayakovsky enthusiastically welcomed both the February and the Bolshevik revolutions of 1917. These great social upheavals seemed to him the sign of long-awaited changes in the world that would bring about the triumph of social and moral justice. Bound up with the revolutions also were his expectations for the new role of art, by which he meant avant-garde art and avant-garde artists, in the new society. Even before the October Revolution, under the Provisional Government, he became passionately involved in political activities. He became a close associate of Gorky in the latter's newspaper *New Life*, which had a distinctly Socialist, though non-Bolshevik, orientation (and thus later fell victim to the Soviet persecutions of the press). He even considered forming his own Futurist Party and putting it forward for the first free elections of the post-Tsarist state.

The weekly newspaper *Art of the Commune*, which began publication in Petrograd in December 1918, reflects the attempts of Mayakovsky's group to win official support for revolutionary culture in the Soviet state. [73] Mayakovsky was one of its founders and a leading member of its editorial board. Devoted to discussing cultural problems in the new socialist world, it had a distinctly partisan character. Noted art and literary critics Viktor Shklovsky and Nikolay Punin and such great artists as Kazimir Malevich and Marc Chagall were among its contributors. Mayakovsky found in it a forum for his verse manifestos, including "It's Too Early To Rejoice," which appeared in the December 7th issue and drew particularly harsh criticism from the Communist Party apparatus. The poem called for a battle against all the old aesthetic values and for a radical break with the classics in the new revolutionary state. The Party officials' displeasure with the philosophy of *Art of the Commune* doomed it to an early demise. Only nineteen issues were published.

The Futurists' bid to become the official, state-supported art movement, in short, was met by the Soviet regime with suspicion and disdain. This rebuff embittered Mayakovsky. After strenuous but unsuccessful attempts to readjust himself and his group to the constantly changing political conditions in Soviet Russia, Mayakovsky shot himself at the age of thirty-six.

**73** *Iskusstvo kommuny* (Art of the Commune), December 7, 1918.

On loan from The Hoover Institution

# IN REVOLUTIONARY STORMS

The October Revolution transformed the Russian literary scene. Writers feverishly grouped and regrouped according to their literary or political orientations. New literary movements sprang up, while older ones faded rapidly away, or found different functions in the new social environment.

Not all of the modernist poets were pleased with the change in the political order. Zinaida Gippius (1869-1945), for example, a founder of the Russian Decadent movement of the 1890s, was a staunch adversary of the Bolshevik regime. Her *Last Verses* sounded an early and eloquent response in poetry to the October Revolution. [74] In December 1919 she and her husband Dmitry Merezhkovsky fled Soviet Russia. They eventually settled in Paris, where their salon, The Green Lamp, was one of the most important intellectual centers of the Parisian émigrés.

Since the first Russian Revolution Gippius had been associated with the revolutionary movement, mainly the Socialist-Revolutionaries. She was particularly close to the notorious revolutionary terrorist Boris Savinkov (1879-1925), who organized the assassinations of Grand Duke Sergey Aleksandrovich and the Tsarist Minister for Internal Affairs, V. Plehve. Under her influence and encouragement, this political assassin turned to writing novels and poetry during the deep ideological crisis of his party in the early 1910s. [75-77] The novels, published under the penname V. Ropshin, created a sensation. During World War I he volunteered for the French Army. Returning to Russia after the February Revolution, he took an active part in Kerensky's Provisional Government. It was primarily through Savinkov that Gippius was kept informed of the behind-the-scenes political activities in the upper levels of Russian society during the weeks just before the Bolsheviks seized power.

After the October Revolution Savinkov headed anti-Bolshevik uprisings in several Russian towns. After emigrating, he became one of the leaders of the anti-Soviet forces abroad. When these activities led him back across the Soviet border in 1924, he was captured and sentenced to long imprisonment. He committed suicide in jail in 1925.

## ■ ALEKSANDR BLOK

A striking case study of the effects of these fundamental changes on an individual poet is the destiny of Aleksandr Blok. In January 1918 he

**74** ZINAIDA GIPPIUS.
*Poslednie stikhi* (The Last Verses). Petersburg, 1918.

**75** V. ROPSHIN
(Boris Savinkov). *Kniga stikhov* (The Book of Poems). Paris, 1931.

Savinkov's only collection of poems was published posthumously in Paris in 1931 with Gippius' preface. She wrote: "I must remark that Savinkov-Ropshin had an amazing quality; I don't know what to call it or how to explain it. 'Talent' is perhaps an understatement; 'genius' is impossible because in his soul, where such enormous contradictions were incessantly clashing, not a single faculty, not even his most brilliant, could approach the sharpness of a genius. This quality, rather, was a kind of magic ability to divine and to grasp that which he needed at any given moment and to instantaneously transform it into his own effective power." Such was certainly the case with Savinkov's poems. Most of them were written in emigration after 1910, during the period of his great disillusionment in revolutionary activities, and vividly reflect these thoughts.

**76** Boris Savinkov to Zinaida Gippius. Autograph letter signed. June 2, 1914.

On loan from The Hoover Institution

The letter, which describes Savinkov's literary affairs, was enclosed in a batch of poems mailed to Gippius. The bundle was intercepted by Russian counterrevolutionary secret police agents in Paris, where Savinkov was under surveillance.

**77** BORIS SAVINKOV.
"Ne diavol li menia lobzaniem smutil?" (Was it the Devil who Disturbed Me with a Kiss?). Autograph manuscript, 1911.

On loan from The Hoover Institution

■ *Item number 78*

wrote his long poem *The Twelve*, the first major poetic response to the Bolshevik coup. Set in Revolutionary Petersburg, it focuses on the story of twelve Red Guard soldiers. It ends with an enigmatic appearance of Jesus Christ at the head of the group, which caused the poem to be interpreted as "blessing" the Revolution.

Sofia Dubnov-Erlich later recalled in her memoirs, published in *Our Age and We* in 1987, that it was

> difficult for the common intellectual to accept this revolution, even if he was a Socialist. That is why we were so stunned when the most tender and subtle poet, who had grown out of Solovievan metaphysics, accepted it and, under his pen, the Second Coming of Christ in Russian literature took place. This was not Tiutchev's Christ who wandered his native land in the guise of a slave, but a Christ who marched at the head of the Red Guard detachment.

But if the poem stunned by its apparent praise for the revolutionary storm, it caused consternation by its audacious style. Blok introduced elements of coarse, language and urban folklore that contrasted sharply with his established image as the poet of the Eternal Feminine—to say nothing of running counter to the principles of Symbolist poetics.

In the events of 1917 and in the Bolshevik coup in particular, Blok saw the inevitable triumph of the elemental forces of history—of the "spirit of music"—over stagnation and human oppression. That is the reason he became one of the first to collaborate with the new regime. "Whatever the differences in personality," he wrote in 1918, "the same music resounds for the intelligentsia as for the Bolsheviks. The intelligentsia have always been drawn toward revolution. The Bolsheviks' decrees are the intelligentsia's symbols. Both are merely slogans, thrown out and demanding to be cultivated."

Blok's quick acceptance of the Bolshevik Revolution, and the appearance of *The Twelve*, isolated the poet from most of his former fellow Symbolists and several close friends. Yet *The Twelve*, Blok's last major work, scored wider popularity than any of his other works. First printed in the newspaper *Banner of Labor* (organ of the Left Socialist-Revolutionaries, who had joined the coalition cabinet), the poem was reissued in countless editions. [78, 79]

Most important among these editions was that undertaken by a small Petrograd private press called "Alkonost," after the bird of sorrow in Russian folklore. [80] Its owner, Samuil Alyansky, had become a publisher because of his great admiration for Blok's poetry. Between 1918 and 1923, a disastrous period for Russian publishing, Alkonost nevertheless managed to bring out a number of Blok's books as well as works by others among the best Symbolist and post-Symbolist poets including Bely, Vyacheslav Ivanov, and Akhmatova. Though *The Twelve* had already been issued as a separate pamphlet by a Left Socialist-Revolutionary publishing house, Alyansky decided to do another edition, this time as a "genuine book," with illustrations. He turned to the young avant-garde artist Jury Annenkov (1889-1974), a friend since secondary-school days. As a painter, Annenkov was then strongly influenced by Cubism. Blok saw and aproved his sketches, and the book appeared in the fall of 1918. It was an enormous success. Three editions followed in rapid succession before the end of the year. Annenkov's drawings for this poem became his most famous artistic work and are now considered inseparable from Blok's text.

The last collection of poems published during Blok's lifetime was *Grey Morning*. [81]

**78** ALEKSANDR BLOK.
*Dvenadtsat* (The Twelve). Sofia, 1920.

Petr Suvchinsky (1892-1985), a Russian émigré literary critic and one of the founders of the "Eurasian" movement in the 1920s, supplied the introductory essay to this edition.

**79** ALEKSANDR BLOK
*Dvenadtsat. Skify* (The Twelve. The Scythians). Paris, [1920].

Illustrated by Nathalie Goncharova and Mikhail Larionov.

**80** ALEKSANDR BLOK.
*Dvenadtsat* (The Twelve). Petersburg, 1918.

Gift of Dr. and Mrs. Boris Wassermann

**81** ALEKSANDR BLOK.
*Sedoe utro* (The Grey Morning). Petersburg, 1920.

Gift of Marie Levinson

This copy is inscribed by the author to Andrey Levinson (1887-1933), a noted literary and dance critic who served with Blok on the editorial board of Gorky's publishing house, "Vsemirnaia Literatura" (World Literature).

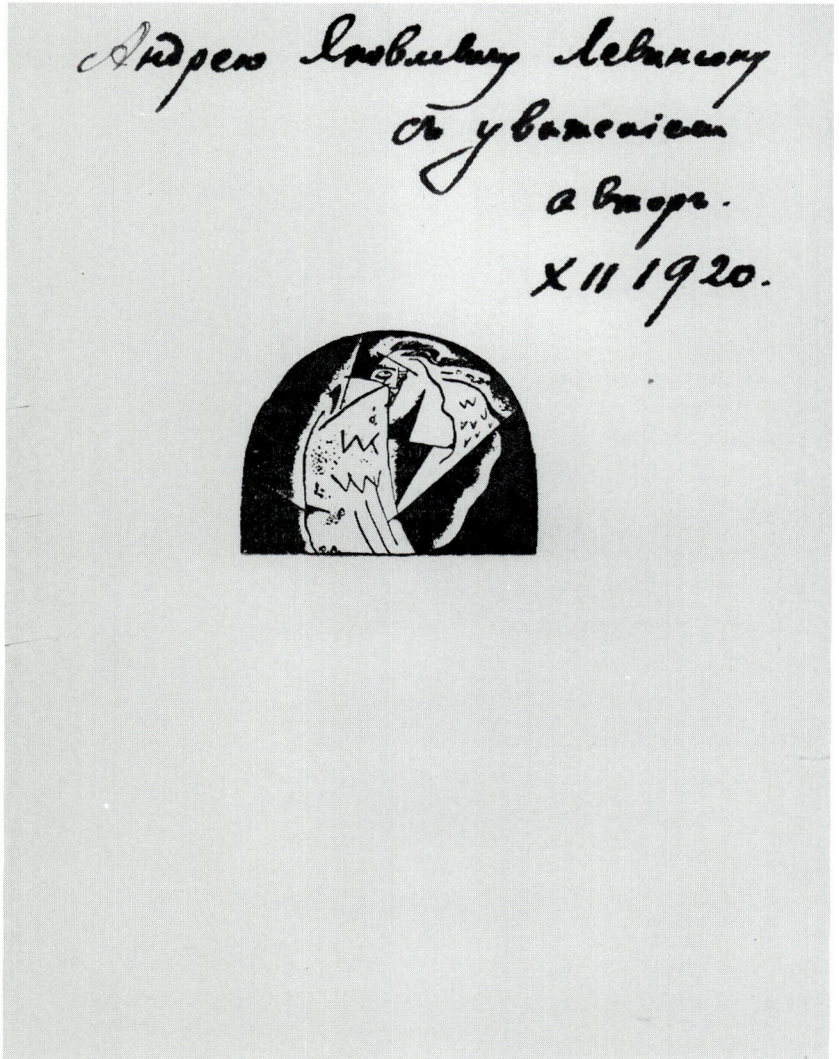

■ Item number 81

# ■ NIKOLAY GUMILEV

Poets in post-Revolutionary Petrograd gravitated mainly toward two opposing poles: Aleksandr Blok, and Nikolay Gumilev. Despite his hatred for the new regime, Gumilev participated in Petrograd's cultural life, lecturing in the History of Arts Institute and leading literary workshops organized for poets from the proletariat. He also served on the editorial board of the World Literature Publishing House, supervising poetry translations with Blok and translations from the French authors with Levinson. With the help of his pupils Georgy Ivanov and Georgy Adamovich, he managed to revive the Guild of Poets. The new Guild's first publishing venture was a miscellany called *The Dragon*. [82] Novice poets contributed to it along with such well-known pre-Revolutionary poets as Blok, Bely, Kuzmin, and Fedor Sologub, and two of the founding members of the Acmeist group, Gumilev and Mandelstam.

By this time Gumilev had become the younger poets' undisputed mentor in all matters of poetic technique and craft. In their eyes, his au-

**82** *Drakon* (The Dragon). Petersburg, 1921.

■ *Item number 80*

Item number 87

thority far outweighed Blok's. Indeed, Gumilev's legacy was to be felt in both Soviet and émigré poetry throughout the 1920s and 1930s. However, the poet himself would die before his time. Arrested on August 3, 1921, and charged with involvement in a counter-revolutionary conspiracy, he and sixty other members of the alleged underground organization were executed by a firing squad on August 21. Gorky's intervention could not save him. Gumilev was only thirty-five.

According to recent revelations in the Soviet Union, Gumilev strongly sympathized with the overthrown monarchy, but never became involved in actual political activity. His only crime was knowing about the plot and failing to inform the secret police.

*The Sounding Shell*, a collection of the verses of Gumilev's pupils, was dedicated to his memory in 1922. [83] In 1923 the members of Gumilev's seminars published another collection, *Literary Evenings*. [84] Among its contributors were such important young poets as Konstantin Vaginov and Vsevolod Rozhdestvensky.

Gumilev's execution coincided with the death of Aleksandr Blok. After his initial euphoria of 1917, Blok became deeply disillusioned and lost hope that the Revolution would bring the "spirit of music" back into the world. He stopped writing poetry. His health rapidly deteriorated, and by the summer of 1921 it became clear that nothing would save him unless he went abroad for medical treatment. Gorky and the People's Commissar for Education, Anatoly Lunacharsky, interceded for him with the Soviet government. At the same time, Vyacheslav Menzhinsky, the deputy head of the Cheka—who in his youth had moved in literary circles—worked to prevent the trip. Permission to travel arrived too late;

**83** *Zvuchashchaia rakovina* (The Sounding Shell). Petersburg, 1922.

**84** *Literaturnye vechera* (Literary Evenings). Petrograd, 1923.

Blok died on August 7th. Within a month Russia had lost two of its greatest poets.

## ■ POETRY AND TERROR

As early as 1918, the Terror and the world of poetry in Soviet Russia collided. In that year the talented young poet Vladimir Paley (1897-1918), son of the Grand Duke Pavel Aleksandrovich, was arrested, sent to internal exile, and executed with other members of the royal family. Before his arrest he was summoned to the office of the chief of the Petrograd Cheka, Moisey Uritsky, and offered a choice—to renounce his father or face persecution. The poet chose the latter. Two poetry collections, published before his death, were highly regarded by many of his contemporaries. [85]

A few weeks after Paley's execution, another young poet, Leonid Kannegiser (1897-1918), assassinated Uritsky. The son of a Petrograd engineer of international repute, Kannegiser belonged to the intellectual elite. He was on close terms with Kuzmin, Esenin, Mandelstam and Georgy Ivanov. Like many of his friends, Kannegiser sympathized with the Revolution and its socialist ideals. But the peace treaty signed by the Bolshevik government with Germany in spring 1918 and the subsequent political repressions angered and disillusioned him. He resolved to commit a terrorist act against the new regime. Kannegiser chose Uritsky as his target because he was determined to contrast himself as a Jew to the new regime's leaders, most of whom were of Jewish origin. He was arrested and, after weeks of interrogation, executed. Official Soviet scholarship tried to eradicate all memory of him and of his poetry. A single small volume, *Leonid Kannegiser*, containing his poems and recollections about him by friends and colleagues, was published in 1928 in Paris. [86]

Yet another casualty of the Civil War was the young Kievan poet and philosopher Vladimir Makkaveysky (1893-1920). Various memoirists speak with deep respect about his extraordinary talents and erudition. His father, Nikolay Makkaveysky (1864-1919), a Professor at the Kiev Theological Academy, wrote a historical monograph on Christ's Passion that strongly influenced Mikhail Bulgakov's novel *The Master and Margarita*. Vladimir Makkaveysky was on friendly terms with Mandelstam, Ilya Erenburg, Grigory Petnikov, and Viktor Shklovsky. In 1920, one literary critic called him, like Mandelstam, a typical representative of Acmeism in poetry. Makkaveysky translated Rainer Maria Rilke's *Marienleben* and Jean Moréas' ballads into Russian as well as Blok's and Vyacheslav Ivanov's poems into French. These French translations appeared in the miscellany *Hermes*, which he edited and published in April 1919 in Kiev, where he also published *On Pierrot, the Murderer*. [87] His monograph on Mallarmé evidently remained unfinished. In the fall of 1919 when the Communist troops were approaching Kiev, he was called to active military duty in the White Army, and was killed in battle near Rostov. His unpublished poems drew historical parallels between contemporary events and the great French Revolution. Included in the exhibit is the typescript of these poems, with the author's autograph corrections. [88]

Although no one was untouched by the Revolution, a few, like Maksimilian Voloshin (1878-1932), tried to remain neutral. Staying in the Crimea throughout this turbulent period, Voloshin took a strictly non-partisan stance, maintaining relations with both sides, and providing refuge to whoever needed it, regardless of politics. As he put it, "One should be a human being and not a citizen in a time of Revolution." What might,

**85** VLADIMIR PALEY.
*Stikhotvoreniia* (Poems). Petrograd, 1916.

**86** *Leonid Kannegiser*. Paris, 1928.

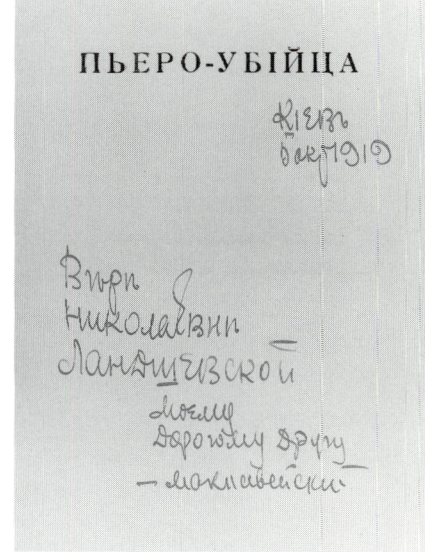

■ *Item number 87*

**87** VLADIMIR MAKKAVEYSKY.
*O Pero-ubiitse* (On Pierrot, the Murderer). Kiev, 1919.

Inscribed by the author to V. Landshevskaya.

**88** VLADIMIR MAKKAVEYSKY.
"Belaia Vandeia" (The White Vandée). Typewritten manuscript, with autograph corrections. 1919.

from this distance, look like a clever strategy for survival was in truth a deeply felt philosophical position, and in maintaining it Voloshin often risked his life. Perhaps it is not surprising, therefore, that Voloshin's Civil War poetry developed extraordinary profundity and lyrical vigor. After the Civil War, Voloshin adopted a similar "above the fray" attitude toward the embattled Soviet and émigré press factions.

Neutrality, however, did not blind him to the horrors around him. His poems describing the bloody butchery of the Revolutionary years, largely unprintable in Soviet Russia, were scattered among émigré literary periodicals of various political persuasions. Voloshin became an "internal émigré." His "Poems on the Terror" appeared in the February 1923 issue of the Berlin periodical *New Russian Book*. [89] They soon reappeared in book form as *Internecine War*, published in Lvov. [90] The author never saw this edition.

Voloshin took part in the activities of an artistic cabaret in Feodosia, which was a meeting place for many notable literati and artists brought to the Crimea by the winds of the Revolution. A slim miscellany, *The Ark*, produced by the Feodosian Literary and Artistic Circle, partially recreates the unique cultural atmosphere that flourished there under the Whites. [91] Mandelstam, Tsvetaeva, Voloshin, and Ilya Erenburg are the most widely known contributors to this collection, which also includes an unauthorized version of a poem by Blok. But other contributors, such as Eduard Bagritsky, Georgy Shengeli, Aleksandr Gatov, and Sofya Parnok, also played an essential role in the literary life of the 1920s. Another contributor was Princess Marie Koudacheff, who wrote poetry in both French and Russian. She later left Russia to marry Romain Rolland.

The miscellany was published by the twenty-one-year-old poet Aleksandr Sokolovsky, whose father was a deputy minister in Hetman Skoropadsky's cabinet. After the White Guard's defeat, Sokolovsky and his parents emigrated. The collection was issued in 1920 in a small run of only one hundred numbered copies.

**89** Maksimilian Voloshin to Aleksandr Iashchenko. Autograph letter signed. November 15, 1922.

On loan from The Hoover Institution

Voloshin's letter to Iashchenko (1877-1934), editor of *Novaia Russkaia kniga* (New Russian Book), authorizes him to publish Voloshin's verses abroad.

**90** MAKSIMILIAN VOLOSHIN. *Usobitsa* (Internecine War). Lvov, 1923.

**91** *Kovcheg* (The Ark). Feodosia, 1920.

# OCTOBER'S CHILDREN
**MAJOR POETIC GROUPS IN THE POST-REVOLUTIONARY YEARS**

Blok's writings of 1917-1918, in particular "The Twelve," were perceived as manifestos of the "Scythian" movement that sprang up in Petersburg shortly before the February Revolution. Politically, the movement was associated with the Left Socialist-Revolutionaries, who joined the Bolsheviks in the Soviet coalition cabinet. Philosophically, the Scythians were inspired by the idea of the uniqueness of Russia. Literary critic Ivanov-Razumnik was the group's main ideologue and Bely was initially the main contributor to its publications. Though this loose literary grouping was extremely short-lived, its doctrine had a long-lasting influence on Russian literature.

## ■ *PEASANT POETS*

The events of 1917 led to an increased role in the Scythian movement for the recently formed group of "peasant" or "people's" poets. The most interesting and influential among them was Nikolay Kliuev (1884-1937), whose appearance in the Petersburg literary salons had caused a stir in 1911-12. Coming from a remote corner of northern Russia, and belonging by birth, religious beliefs, and dialect to the traditional peasantry, Kliuev struck everyone not only by his exotic dress and manners but also by his violent rejection of the modern urban "iron" civilization and its cult of the Machine, which, he maintained, had caused the split between Man and Nature.

Kliuev's message had enormous impact on Blok, who was looking for new writers from among the people. "There is a new Jesus Christ among us," said Blok. "It is Nikolay Kliuev." They had started to correspond in 1907, well before they met in person. Blok introduced Kliuev into the literary circles of Petersburg and Moscow and helped him publish his first volumes of poetry, which were an immediate success. Various literary factions courted the new celebrity, but Kliuev was trying to establish his own independent group of poets with social backgrounds and views similar to his own. This plan materialized in 1915 when he met Sergey Esenin. The poetry of Kliuev's group featured stylized folklore genres, symbols from Rusian peasant Christianity, and elements of rural language in all its exotic freshness.

Kliuev and other peasant poets enthusiastically welcomed the Bolshevik Revolution. They interpreted it in messianic terms and looked forward to a peasant paradise. The Revolution embodied for them a complete "transfiguration," a rejuvenation of life. This interpretation seemed akin to the dreams of the second-generation Symbolists about the transformation of life that would, among other things, bridge the chasm between the intelligentsia and the people. Hence the close cooperation between the Symbolists Blok and Bely and the peasant poets immediately after the Bolshevik coup.

In 1918 Kliuev wrote a cycle of poems praising Vladimir Lenin. These poems, among the earliest of a host of such paeans composed after the October Revolution, were unique in endowing Lenin's image with distinctly "peasant" features rather than glorifying him as a proletarian leader. They appeared in Kliuev's collection *The Song Book*, published in two volumes on direct order of Education Commissar Lunacharsky. [92] The Lenin poems also appeared in Kliuev's book *Song of the Sunbearer*. [93]

In 1918 Kliuev, alone of all the peasant poets, became a member of the Communist Party. Two years later his religious views were found incompatible with Party membership, and he was expelled. By the late 1920s his ideal of a rural Russia untouched by modern civilization came under fierce attack from official quarters. With collectivization of the countryside under way, he and his closest ally Sergey Klychkov (1889-1940) [94] were accused of promoting the views of the so-called *kulaks* (well-to-do farmers targeted for extermination by the First Five-year plan). Publication of their poems was prohibited. Like other peasant poets, Kliuev and Klychkov fell victim to the Stalinist purges of the late 1930s.

## ■ IMAGISTS

Sergey Esenin (1895-1925), who always called Kliuev his teacher in poetry, deserted the camp of peasant poets and broke with the Scythian ideology in late 1918. In Moscow, together with Vadim Shershenevich, Riurik Ivnev, and Anatoly Mariengof, he formed a new literary movement, Imagism, that was to play an essential role in this early post-Revolutionary period. The Imagists' first manifesto, published in January 1919, was signed also by two avant-garde painters, Georgy Yakulov and Boris Erdman. The Imagists aligned themselves primarily with the aesthetic principles of Futurism. Two of the new group's founders—Shershenevich and Ivnev—had been active contributors to various Futurist publications. Mariengof's poetry was in many respects strikingly similar to the "urbanist" works of Burliuk. The Imagists' poems as well as their manifestos closely resembled those of the early Futurists in style. Like the Futurists, the Imagists called for "freeing poetry from the shackles of grammar" and "turning the word upside down." Even their public behavior, with its open aggressiveness, garish self-advertisement, and eagerness to shock and scandalize, was reminiscent of the Futurists.

Significant differences did exist between them, however. The Imagists detected two contradictory strains in Futurist poetry: on the one hand, Mayakovsky, leader of the movement, flouting all its public slogans and theoretical pronouncements by his commitment to content; and on the other hand, his extremist opponents, with their transrational language. The Imagists now advanced the notion of a poetic text as a "catalog of images" following each other haphazardly, so that ideally, each poem could be read not only from beginning to end but also in the other direc-

**92** NIKOLAY KLIUEV.
*Pesnoslov* (The Song Book).
Petrograd, 1919.

**93** NIKOLAY KLIUEV.
*Pesnia solntsenostsa* (Song of the Sunbearer).
Berlin, 1920.

**94** SERGEY KLYCHKOV.
*Potaennyi sad* (Secret Garden).
Moscow, 1918.

This publishing house, the Moscow Labor Artel of the Artists of the Word, was affiliated with the bookshop organized by Esenin and Klychkov in fall of 1918.

tion, and still be comprehensible. In short, the Imagists used rational language, but undermined traditional ideas of content. The concept of "image" thus took aim simultaneously at both wings of the Futurist camp.

At first, the new group enjoyed the support of the Soviet officials, partly because one of its founders, Riurik Ivnev, was Lunacharsky's personal secretary. In the most difficult months of the Civil War, when the nationalization of private enterprise and severe paper shortages virtually halted publishing in Soviet Russia, the Imagists managed to publish several anthologies and works by individual poets, such as Mariengof's *Pastry Shop of the Suns* [95], most of them under the imprint of their own publishing house. They even published poets who did not share their views or sign their manifestos—Bely, Khlebnikov, Pasternak, and later, Osip Mandelstam. Imagism seemed to offer a real alternative to Mayakovsky's and other Futurists' insistence on subordinating literary activities to the goals of the Soviet state. The Imagists insisted on art's independence, and valued technique above ideology.

*Reality* was their first group publication. [96] It came out in late February of 1919, but it had been put together several months earlier. Along

**95** ANATOLY MARIENGOF. *Konditerskaia solnts* (The Pastry-Shop of the Suns). Moscow, 1919.

**96** *Iav* (Reality). Moscow, 1919.

■ *Item number 96*

with the Imagist leaders Mariengof, Esenin, Ivnev, and Shershenevich, its contributors included poets who did not formally belong to the new group—Bely, Kamensky, and Pasternak. The poems, especially Mariengof's, infuriated Party officials. *Pravda* fiercely attacked the collection, and Ivnev was forced to publicly renounce his membership in the group.

The group was soon joined by a minor but prolific poet, Aleksandr Kusikov (1896-1977). Though born to an Armenian family, he always claimed that he descended from Circassians (non-Indo-European-speaking people of the Caucusus). His books, such as *The Mirror of Allah*, added a distinctly Oriental flavor to the group's poetry as he combined Muslim themes and images with Christian ones. [97] Kusikov's poem, "Al-Kadr," appeared in 1921 in *The Starry Bull*. [98] This collection, which also included Esenin's lyrical poetry, was produced on a printing press aboard the train of an unsuspecting Trotsky. In January 1922 Kusikov left Russia for Berlin, and two years later moved to Paris. In both places he cooperated with pro-Soviet periodicals. Later he took anti-Soviet positions, but nevertheless avoided contact with the émigré Russian community.

Between 1918 and 1922 the Imagist movement appeared the most influential and attractive to young poets gravitating toward the avantgarde. In Petrograd, three young poets, Grigory Shmerelson, Semen Polotsky, and Vladimir Richiotti, formed a sub-group of the Imagists that published a number of poetry collections. The first, appearing in April 1922 under the imprint of the Crucified Harlequin, was Shmerelson's *The Gloom of the City*. [99] A poet and journalist, Shmerelson was born in 1901 in Nizhny-Novgorod and made his literary debut there. He disappeared from the literary scene in the late 1920s and died in the 1940s (the exact date of his death remains unknown).

Esenin's active involvement with the Imagists surprised many of his contemporaries—so different were his aesthetic principles and so incomparably more powerful was his poetic gift. His decision to join stemmed from his deep disillusionment with Blok and Kliuev, who had previously influenced him most. He came to feel they devoted too little attention to the formal aspects of poetic technique. However, the Imagists' themes and values, especially their distinctly "urbanist" orientation, were never really his, either. He collaborated with the group because he felt that "peasant" poetry had no more chance to survive in the "iron" age than did an idealized rural Russia in the new cultural environment. In the poem that opened his collection *Treriadnitsa*, he wrote, "I am the last village poet." [100] The new group seemed to offer a way out of the impasse. However, Esenin's effort to adjust to post-Revolutionary reality failed. Esenin soon felt as alien within Imagism as the Imagists felt within Soviet literature. Their attempt to revive the spirit of revolt characteristic of early Futurism was intolerable to the new state. It was Esenin who, together with the chief theoretician of Imagism, Ivan Gruzinov, announced in *Pravda* the disbanding of the group in February 1924.

Esenin's inner conflict between his love for the doomed world of the "peasant hut" and his desire to accept the new post-Revolutionary values led to suicide in 1925. Esenin's incompatibility with the emerging Soviet culture was laid bare soon thereafter as the government unleashed its campaign against "Eseninianism." The works of this popular poet were blamed for inspiring the wave of "hooliganism" that seemed to be sweeping Soviet cities. For several decades Esenin's poems were rarely reprinted, and indeed an attempt was made to obliterate his name from the

**97** ALEKSANDR KUSIKOV. *Zerkalo Allakha* (The Mirror of Allah). Moscow, 1918.

In this, Kusikov's first, pre-imagist work, the Revolution is recalled in the poem "Eto Bylo v Moskve" (This Happened in Moscow), dated November 1917.

**98** ALEKSANDR KUSIKOV AND SERGEY ESENIN. *Zvezdny byk* (The Starry Bull). Moscow, 1921.

**99** GRIGORY SHMERELSON. *Goroda khmur* (The Gloom of the City). Petersburg, 1922.

**100** SERGEY ESENIN. *Treriadnitsa*. [Moscow, 1920].

This copy is the first edition, which appeared with no mention of the place or date of publication. The next edition was issued later the same year by the "Zlak" publishing house.

official annals of Soviet literature. It was primarily in émigré literature that the cult of Esenin persisted. His works continued to be printed in Berlin and Paris. [101, 102] The rehabilitation of Esenin's legacy in the 1950s was associated with the steady rise of nationalistic tendencies in Soviet culture. His poetry, along with Kliuev's, is regarded today as the embodiment of the Russian national character.

### ■ PROLETARIAN POETS

"Proletarian" poetry, proceeding from an assumption of the importance of class (family origin and social background) in literature, appeared, like its "peasant" counterpart, shortly before 1917. Proletarian literature at first received strong encouragement and support from Gorky and such unorthodox Bolshevik functionaries as Lunacharsky and Aleksandr Bogdanov. The October Revolution gave rise to a far-flung network of "proletarian culture" (Proletcult) associations that were independent of the Communist Party. They soon became the most powerful of the unofficial cultural and educational organizations. Realizing the potential danger of a formidable rival enjoying such great influence on the masses, the Party decided to take Proletcult activities under its control in 1920.

Early Proletcult poets saw the Bolshevik Revolution as a cosmic cataclysm, the first in a series of events that would lead inevitably to new social relationships based on justice and equality. The dominant note of their lyrics was exultation. They painted recent historical events larger than life, and praised the accomplishments of industrial civilization in pompous and high-flown language. Factory workers were the main subjects and protagonists of their poetry, and their goal was to encourage such semi-literate workers to start writing.

In style, the Proletcult poets proved to be imitators of the early Symbolists Balmont and Briusov. This dependence on the Symbolists was particularly ironic in view of the fact that the Proletarian poets repeatedly criticized the "bourgeois aesthetes." In the end, the Proletcults were unable to prove the artistic originality of their poetry, or to produce any first-rate writers like Kliuev or Esenin. However, several early Proletarian authors, such as Mikhail Gerasimov (1889-1939), Vladimir Kirillov (1890-1943), Vasily Aleksandrovsky (1897-1934) [103], Nikolay Poletaev (1889-1935) [104], and Vasily Kazin (1898-1981), had genuine talent and a sincere devotion to poetry and evoked a keen interest and sympathy among the Symbolist poets Blok, Bely, and Khodasevich. The latter two even taught at seminars arranged for beginning proletarian writers.

### ■ VAPP

Along with some genuine, if minor poets, "proletarian literature" attracted a variety of ambitious literary hacks who joined the ruling Communist Party and called themselves proletarian writers. They were to play an essential role in Soviet cultural policy. Beginning in the early 1920s, they formed the core of the All-Union Association of Proletarian Writers (VAPP). This organization, fully controlled by the Party apparatus, was proclaimed the advance guard of the nascent Soviet literature. The Proletcult poets of the first years of the Revolution were pushed aside by these latecomers, who were gradually entrusted with the immense administrative power of the VAPP. The VAPP leaders also took an inimical stance toward various factions of the non-Party intelligentsia (whom Trotsky called the "fellow-travelers of the Revolution"). This change in cultural politics greatly troubled Gorky, who had lived abroad since 1921.

Semen Rodov (1893-1968) stood out as a fanatical Party watchdog in

**101** SERGEY ESENIN.
*Triptikh* (Triptych). Berlin, 1920.

**102** SERGEY ESENIN.
*Moi put* (My Path) Paris, 1926.

The work was issued posthumously by the "Ocharovannyi Strannik" (Enchanted Wanderer) publishing house.

**103** VASILY ALEKSANDROVSKY.
*Vosstanie* (The Uprising). Moscow, 1919.

This work was the first in a series published by the journal *Gorn* (Furnace).

**104** NIKOLAY POLETAEV.
*Stikhi* (Poems). Moscow, 1919.

the VAPP until 1925, when his demagogical attacks against the "fellow travelers" were silenced by Khodasevich. Vladislav Khodasevich had left Soviet Russia in 1922 but still retained his Soviet citizenship and, being a close friend of Gorky, lived for some time in his household. Backed by Gorky, he wrote and published in the left-wing émigré newspaper *Dni* (Days) an article exposing Rodov's politically dubious past, his activities in the period just before and just after the 1917 Bolshevik coup. Khodasevich mentioned, among other things, Rodov's first poetry collection, *My Sowing*. [105] The strong Zionist sympathies of this work were doubly embarrassing for Rodov in view of the harsh anti-Zionist persecutions the Soviet Union had undertaken since the mid-1920s. As a result of this and several others of Khodasevich's émigré publications, his Soviet passport was revoked, and the door was closed against his return. Rodov and his comrades were removed from the VAPP leadership, but unfortunately, the newly appointed leaders were no less orthodox and zealous than their predecessors. The change by no means inhibited the VAPP in its fierce attacks against all "deviationists" from the Party line.

## ■ KOMSOMOL POETS

Beginning in the early 1920s, the Proletarian camp in literature was reinforced by the emerging Komsomol (Communist Youth League) group of poets. The most remarkable among them was Aleksandr Bezymensky (1898-1973). Strange as it now seems, he was seriously regarded as a rival to Mayakovsky, both in power of lyrical expression and in popularity. As to political orthodoxy, he had no peers. His work, without exception, was blatantly propagandist and fully subordinated to the political goals of the government. [106, 107] Like Demyan Bedny and Mayakovsky, he limited his poetry-writing mainly to rhymed newspaper editorials. Bezymensky's loyalty won official approval. His most famous work, *So That's How Life Smells*, was published in 1925 with a preface by Trotsky, which said in part, "Of all our poets who wrote about the Revolution, for the Revolution, concerning the Revolution, Bezymensky approaches it the most organically, for he is flesh of its flesh, the son of the Revolution, an October child." [108]

In the 1930s Bezymensky's influence and popularity waned. Nikolay Bukharin's famous speech at the First Congress of Soviet Writers in 1934 singled him out as an example of how poets who follow the changing political course of the State too faithfully lose their artistic identity and integrity. In 1937, Bezymensky was publicly accused of having a Trotskyite oppositionist past, and expelled from the Party and the Union of Soviet Writers. Such accusations were often the first step toward arrest, but for unknown reasons he escaped. Though he was soon readmitted to both organizations and allowed to publish again, he never regained his old reputation and fame.

**105** SEMEN RODOV.
*Moi sev* (My Sowing). Moscow, 1918.

**106** ALEKSANDR BEZYMENSKY.
*Oktiabrskie zori* (October Dawns). Kazan, 1920.

The second edition of Bezymensky's book of lyrics was published by the Kazan Province Committee of the Russian Communist Youth League.

**107** ALEKSANDR BEZYMENSKY.
*Iuny proletarii: Zhizn Miti* (The Young Proletarian: Mitia's Life). Astrakhan, 1919.

*The Young Proletarian* went through several editions in various provincial cities. The present copy, sponsored by the Russian Telegraph Agency, was printed aboard the "agitational steamboat" of the All-Union Central Executive Committee.

**108** ALEKSANDR BEZYMENSKY.
*Tak pakhnet zhizn* (So That's How Life Smells). Leningrad, 1925.

# TAKING STOCK
**POETRY IN THE NEP PERIOD**

1922 was a year of great expectation and disillusionment. The New Economic Policy (NEP) legitimized private enterprise after a four-year freeze during the Civil War. This move caused mixed reactions among the literary intelligentsia, many of whom had welcomed the Revolution and were distressed by the abandonment of its lofty ideals and the unimaginable concessions to the old order. But the resulting economic revival rapidly normalized cultural life. New publishing and printing houses mushroomed, and new periodicals, miscellanies, and individual poetry collections followed in rapid succession. Short-lived literary groups sprang up, only to disappear soon after their first organizational meetings or after the publication of their first manifestos.

The new social situation called for reevaluating the role of various forces in the literary scene. It became easier to see which of the once-influential literary schools were approaching their eclipse and which of the new ones seemed on the rise.

In his article in *Press and Revolution* (1922), Briusov wrote that the "Symbolists entered the age of the Revolution like a defeated army which had lost many of its commanders and in the last few years had failed to acquire a single valuable ally." And, indeed, Blok died in 1921; Balmont, Gippius, and Merezhkovsky emigrated; and Bely went to Berlin for an indefinite stay. Vycheslav Ivanov seemed to be moving toward an academic career in the provinces. Briusov had so radically changed his lyric style to accommodate Futurist innovations that he could hardly be considered a Symbolist any longer. Other symbolist poets attracted no attention from the younger generation.

Futurism, in all its various factions, including Imagism, exerted the strongest influence on poetry at this time, as even Lunacharsky acknowledged in 1922. However, this situation soon changed. In 1922 the movement lost its most important member, Velemir Khlebnikov, whose artistic works and theories contributed so greatly to the radical transformation of the language of poetry. [109-111] He was thirty-six at the time of his death.

**109** VELEMIR KHLEBNIKOV. *Zangezi.* Moscow, 1922.

Khlebnikov attributed this work to the syncretic genre he called "supertale." The text was composed of relatively autonomous sections linked by the appearance of a single character, Zangezi, the philosopher. Zangezi sums up Khlebnikov's ideas on the "language of gods" and the governing role of numbers in history. The work was staged in Petrograd in May 1923, directed by Vladimir Tatlin (1885-1953), one of the great painters of the Russian avant-garde.

**110** *Russkoe iskusstvo* (Russian Art), 1923:1.

This issue includes Tatlin's sketches of the stage decorations for the production of *Zangezi*.

**111** VELEMIR KHLEBNIKOV. *Stikhi* (Poems). Moscow, 1922.

Published by the avant-garde artist Petr Miturich (1887-1956), Poems appeared shortly after the poet's death. It opens with Vyacheslav Ivanov's poem written in 1909 and addressed to Khlebnikov, who was then attending the "Academy of Verse" organized by Ivanov. This obviously was meant to emphasize the non-futurist elements of Khlebnikov's art. The short memoir by his sister Vera Khlebnikova (1891-1941) also indicates the dissatisfaction and bitterness the poet's family held for his Futurist cohorts.

### ■ BORIS PASTERNAK

It was just then that Boris Pasternak's (1890-1960) third book of poetry, *My Sister, Life*, appeared. [112] Most of the poems in this collection had been written between 1917 and 1919, and had been circulating in handwritten form for some time; they were now first published in May of 1922 in Moscow by Grzhebin. The book was reprinted several months later in Berlin. No other book of poems in post-Revolutionary Russia had such a deep effect on contemporary poetry. Subtitled "The Summer of 1917," the book was an intensely lyrical and subjective response to the Revolution. Paradoxically, the content of the book was almost entirely confined to traditional themes—love, nature, poetry. The single reference to a concrete event occurs in the poem "Spring Rain," which mentions Aleksandr Kerensky's speech delivered at the Bolshoi Theater in Moscow at the height of his popularity, on May 26, 1917. Though this poem had appeared as early as the fall of 1917 in the pro-Kerensky biweekly *Path of Liberation*, Kerensky did not read it until 1924. Shown Pasternak's book in Prague by Marina Tsvetaeva, he was deeply moved by the poem.

■ *Item number 109*

**112** BORIS PASTERNAK.
*Sestra moia zhizn* (My Sister, Life).
Berlin, 1922.

рис. Юрій Завадскій.

## ЭДМОНДЪ КИНЪ

Лондонскій вѣтеръ срываетъ мокрый брезентъ балагана.
Низкая сцена. Свѣчи. Холстъ размалеванъ, какъ міръ.
Ложи встаютъ горбомъ. Въ райкѣ напоръ урагана,
Гонитъ за гибелью въ небо пьяныхъ актеровъ Шекспиръ.

Макбетъ по вереску мчится. Конь взлетаетъ на воздухъ.
Мокрыя пряди волосъ лезутъ въ больные глаза,
Вѣдьмы гадаютъ о царствахъ. Ямбъ діалога громоздокъ.
Шестъ съ головой Короля торчитъ, разодравъ небеса.

Вѣдьмы летятъ и поютъ. Занавѣсъ бѣдный задвинутъ.
Въ клочья разорвана страсть. Отхлынулъ въ ночь ураганъ.
Кассу считаетъ директоръ. Полночь. Столъ опрокинутъ.
Леди къ спутникамъ жмутся. Запертъ пустой балаганъ.

П. Антокольскій

Облака подъ мертвымъ вѣтромъ загибались,
Разлагались въ замогильной сарабандѣ.
Выростали многоярусные кубы.
И слезились въ переулкахъ фонари.
И прохожіе другъ другу улыбались,
Шулера сходились въ карточные клубы.
И сдвигались,—и сдвигались по командѣ
Облака, какъ неподвижные драпри,

Черный вечеръ выглядѣлъ сутулымъ
Музыкантомъ въ старомодной разлетайкѣ.
И казалось,—и казалось онъ тоскуетъ
Въ облакахъ своихъ, какъ пьяный въ кабакѣ:
Брякнетъ въ изступленьи о полъ стуломъ,
И быть можетъ, и быть можетъ безъ утайки
Длинноногой тѣни спьяну растолкуетъ,
Какъ натягиваютъ струны на смычкѣ.

Антокольскій

■ Item number 114

No other direct reference to political circumstances or events appeared in *My Sister, Life*. Precisely for that reason, Pasternak's fellow poets and other sophisticated readers regarded it as the profoundest expression of the Revolution's character. Toward the end of his life Pasternak returned to 1917 in his novel *Doctor Zhivago*. Despite several decades separating the novel from the poems, the similarities in attitude toward the Revolution in the two works are striking.

*My Sister, Life* engendered countless and usually unsuccessful imitations. It was a favorite book for such diverse poets as Mayakovsky, Mandelstam, Tsvetaeva, and Aseev. Among the young poets influenced by Pasternak, two stood out: Pavel Antokolsky (1896-1978) and Nikolay Tikhonov (1896-1979). Antokolsky's first collection, *Poems*, appeared in 1922. [113, 114] Tikhonov's *The Horde* was published the same year by a young group of Petersburg poets, the *Ostrovitiane* (Islanders), who were followers of Gumilev. [115] Both poets later played significant roles in Soviet literature.

The appearance of *My Sister, Life* raised the question of Pasternak's relation to contemporary literary movements. Critics had trouble placing him. On the one hand, his ties with Mayakovsky's Futurist group seemed as close as they had been with the Centrifuge before 1917. On the other hand, many of the poet's statements and characteristic features of his poetry were at variance with Futurist slogans and aesthetic ideas from both before and after the Revolution. Pasternak's literary position puzzled his contemporaries as much as did his difficult and esoteric lyrics.

## ■ LEF

Pasternak returned home in March 1923 after nine months in Germany, disappointed with the émigré literature he found there. He decided to join LEF, headed by his close friends Mayakovsky and Aseev, whose work he much admired.

However, sharp disagreements soon arose with other LEF members, and in 1927 Pasternak abandoned its ranks. (So did also another great artist of the time-avant-garde filmmaker Sergey Eisenstein. The roots of this conflict lay in LEF ideology. One of its tenets, advanced by Aseev, confined the artist in the new socialist society to carrying out projects commissioned by Party and state officials. Agitprop verse written for newspapers—what Mandelstam called harnessing the swallows into legions—was considered closest to this ideal and thus the most important of all poetic genres. It was just the sort of thing that Pasternak consistently avoided, despite seeming to share with LEF a reverence for the Russian Revolution.

LEF also pronounced on the role of artistic imagination in the new culture. Before the Revolution, art and society were antagonists, and artists were forced to seek refuge in the products of their imagination. With the the new political order, however, LEF argued, harmonious relations prevailed; thus writers should turn to the "literature of fact," such as sketches, memoirs, and biographies, rather than novels or poems, and artists to photography and documentary films instead of "easel painting." Thus the avant-garde artists had come full circle: if at the start they called for art forms devoid of any real-life content, they now preferred those forms most carefully documenting reality. Taken to its extreme, of course, the "literature of fact" would unavoidably destroy art. No wonder that the poetry of Aseev and Mayakovsky showed clear signs of withering in the course of the 1920s.

**113** PAVEL ANTOKOLSKY.
*Stikhotvoreniia* (Poems). Moscow, 1922.

**114** *Sorokonozhka* (Centipede), Moscow, 1918.

On loan from The Hoover Institution

Antokolsky's poems first appeared in this short-lived journal.

**115** NIKOLAY TIKHONOV.
*Orda: Stikhi 1920-1921* (The Horde: The Poems of 1920-1921). Petersburg, 1922.

# ■ VLADIMIR MAYAKOVSKY

In his zeal to have his group recognized as the representatives of official art, Mayakovsky did not hesitate to abandon both the values and the rebellious spirit of the original Futurist doctrine. The more clearly the Soviet officials rejected avant-garde poetry and art, the more eagerly Mayakovsky strove to please them.

In 1925 he traveled to Mexico and the United States. The cult of the machine, of modern technical civilization, had been a central motif in the Futurists' urbanist poetry. Mayakovsky's trip to America stemmed, as he put it, from the desire to test his own previous calls for the "Americanization" of Russian life. His old friend Burliuk, the "Father of Russian Futurism," had settled in New York by that time and helped organize Mayakovsky's tour. Their reunion prompted the New York publication in October 1925 of Mayakovsky's *The Sun on a Visit to Mayakovsky*, illustrated by Burliuk. [116] This long poem, written in 1919, gave friendlier and more optimistic overtones to the heliomachian idea of Futurist poetry, and provided a new twist to the treatment of the solar theme in the early writings of such Russian Symbolists as Balmont and Bely.

It was in America that Mayakovsky publicly announced his break with Futurism, claiming that its ideology was incompatible with the building of socialism. "From now on I am against futurism," he insisted. "From

**116** VLADIMIR MAYAKOVSKY. *Solntse v gostiakh u Maiakovskogo* (The Sun on a Visit to Mayakovsky). New York, 1925.

Its title was invented by Burliuk, to a large extent still faithful to the ethos of early Futurist performances. The author himself was going to limit the title to a somewhat more modest "The Sun" and expressed his displeasure to Burliuk.

■ *Item number 116*

now on I will fight against it." Instead of praising the machine civilization *in toto*, as before, the LEF group now called for "judicious regulation," organization, and self-discipline. Those slogans reflected the desire of the post-Revolutionary Futurists to dissociate themselves from their rebellious past.

## ■ OBERIU

That is why the LEF refused to allow the young radical Leningrad poets to join its ranks. Formed in the mid-1920s, the Leningrad group was the last avant-garde organization to appear in the Soviet Union. It moved from purely transrational poetry toward what would become known in the West as the literature of the absurd.

The group entered the literary scene as the "Left Wing" but later changed its name to "Oberiu" (Association for Realist Art), using the term "realism" in Malevich's sense. (Malevich claimed that his abstract art was more real than what was usually called realist art.) Daniil Kharms (1906-1942) and Aleksandr Vvedensky (1904-1941) were its founders and leaders. They were joined by an older poet, Aleksandr Tufanov (1877-ca.1940), who stood outside any literary school, stubbornly promoting transrational poetry at a time when it was becoming increasingly unacceptable in the new society. Tufanov's theory was spelled out concisely in a manifesto introducing his *Ancient Novgorod's River Pirates*. [117] Kharms' and Vvedensky's experimental poetry found its way into print only twice during their lifetimes, when their poems were included in two miscellanies published by the Leningrad Union of Poets in 1926-27. [118] Not until the late 1960s did Oberiu's activities become known to literary historians. Once rediscovered, these writers began to be widely published and studied, though mainly outside the Soviet Union.

Oberiu was unacceptable to Mayakovsky's group because it rejected the idea of art as servant to the state and the calls to write agitprop verse and "literature of fact." Aseev's major work of the mid-20s, his epic poem *Semen Proskakov*, perfectly exemplified the state-approved writing that Oberiu rejected. [119] The author himself described this work as verse footnotes to documentary materials on the Civil War in the Russian Far East. Recounting the story of a Red guerilla captured and executed by Admiral Kolchak's forces, drawing heavily on archival sources and memoirs of witnesses, the poem was generally regarded as an artistic failure.

Aseev remained Mayakovsky's most loyal ally throughout the crisis that plagued LEF beginning in the summer of 1928. This crisis was both internal and external. The group, which had originally attracted the best poets of the period, was less and less able to create works of real artistic value. Indeed, it seemed to be proving its own doctrine that art would wither away under socialism. No less important were certain external forces. Toward the end of the 1920s the Party enforced its new literary policy, aimed at bringing all literary activities under its day-to-day control. No literary groups except the VAPP were to be tolerated.

In January of 1930, Mayakovsky decided to join VAPP, even though his past literary career and his fundamental artistic tastes and views cried out against it. Mayakovsky's most faithful friends, including Aseev, now turned away from him. The greatest poet of the epoch was condemned to excruciating loneliness, as most of the active figures in the literary and cultural scene boycotted him. On April 14, only two months after joining VAPP, Mayakovsky shot himself. If Esenin's death seemed consonant

**117** ALEKSANDR TUFANOV. *Ushkuiniki* (Ancient Novgorod River-Pirates). Leningrad, 1927.

Tufanov signed his introduction, "Osnovy zaumnogo mirooquqeniia" (Fundamentals of the Transrational World Outlook), in the same fashion as Khlebnikov: "President of the Terrestrial Globe, Aleksandr Tufanov."

**118** *Koster* (Bonfire). Leningrad, 1927.

The second of the two collections published by the Leningrad Union of Poets, *Bonfire* includes the poems of Kharms and Vvedensky.

**119** NIKOLAY ASEEV. *Semen Proskakov*. Moscow, 1928.

with his bohemian lifestyle and with his poetry's motifs, Mayakovsky's seemed contrary to his heroic nature. His death marked the demise of modernist culture, with its inherently revolutionary tendencies and ideals, in Soviet Russia.

## ■ CONSTRUCTIVISTS

The Constructivist group (1922-30) was, like Imagism, an offshoot of the Futurist movement and an attempt to discover an alternative way of combining avant-garde artistic values with political loyalty. It rejected both the LEF slogan of transforming art into industry and Mayakovsky's early tendency toward intensely emotional lyricism. The Constructivists' artistic goal was to create poems that would be highly rational and well-organized on all levels. Constructivism did not reject the artistic devices employed by the Symbolists, Futurists, or Imagists. Rather, it considered all of them equally usable for its purposes and as consecutive stages on the way to synthesis. The Constructivist group was highly heterogeneous and unstable. Only the work of its leader, Ilya Selvinsky (1899-1968), imparted some degree of unity to the movement.

Selvinsky had an unusual background. His family were *krimchaks*—the tiny Crimean minority of Tatar-speaking Jews. In 1905, when the Crimean *pogroms* began, Selvinsky's father sent his children out of the country to the safety of Constantinople. Ilya studied there in a Muslim ele-

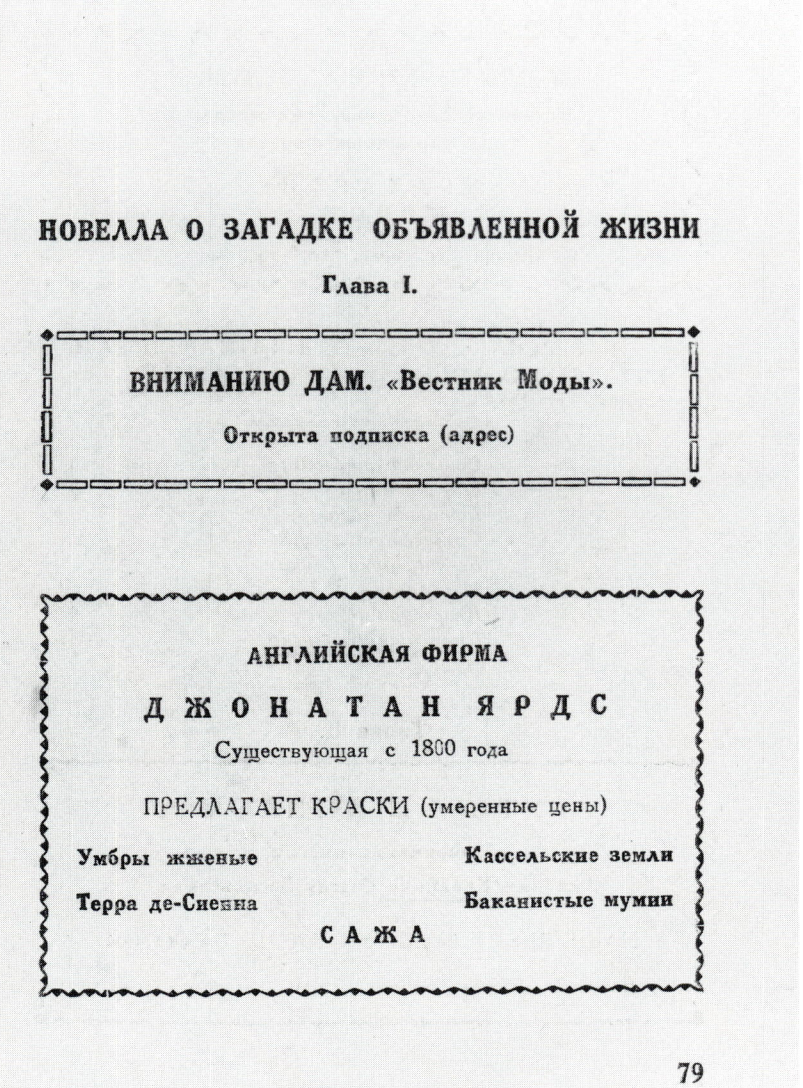

■ *Item number 121*

Item number 122

mentary school before returning to Russia. As early as middle school, he wrote poetry and experimented with meter and style. During the Civil War he fought for the Reds.

Selvinsky's principal contribution to the literature of the '20s was in the realm of epic poetry rather than in the lyric. [120] His long poem *Ulyalaevism* (1924), devoted to the Civil War guerillas, was a great success and placed him among the leading poets of the decade. Once Mayakovsky half-jokingly said that he should have written this work rather than Selvinsky. All attempts to lure the Constructivists into an alliance with the LEF failed. Selvinsky was dismayed at the idea of writing propagandist newspaper verse, and more inclined to experiment with form than the LEF poets would have allowed. Selvinsky's experimental poems appeared in his collection *Setting Records*. [121] In audacity of artistic technique, Selvinsky's later work would never surpass these early poems.

Selvinsky's verse novel, *Notes of a Poet*, offers a broad overview of contemporary literature. [122] Written under the name of another poet, Evgeny Ney, it is an autobiography in disguise. Its first canto ends with an aphorism on the nature of relations between life and art: "The Revolution came in order to enable Blok to create 'The Twelve.'" Its fourth canto imitates in verse the minutes of a Constructivist meeting. The fifth canto represents the "posthumous" edition of Ney's lyrical poetry. As befits such a book, it is supplied with a "biographical sketch" of the late poet and his portrait. However, Ney's poem appears in the oval frame instead of his picture.

The group's third miscellany, *Business*, published in 1929, was its last collective volume. [123] It appeared shortly before the fierce official campaign against Selvinsky and his followers, who were accused of "formalism" and ideological deviations. These accusations coincided with the government's frontal attacks on all forms of artistic independence. On the day of Mayakovsky's suicide, the Constructivists disbanded. "Constructivism did not die of natural causes," Selvinsky later reported, it "was beheaded." Thus it shared the fate of LEF and all the other schools of the Russian literary avant-garde in the Soviet epoch.

**120** ILYA SELVINSKY. *Ranny Selvinsky* (Early Selvinsky). Moscow, 1929.

**121** ILYA SELVINSKY. *Recordy* (Setting Records). Moscow, 1931.

In "Novella o zagadke obiavlennoi zhizni" (The Novella about the Riddle of Life Announced) Selvinsky's verse text imitates newspaper advertisements.

**122** ILYA SELVINSKY. *Zapiski poeta* (Notes of a Poet). Moscow, 1928.

**123** *Biznes* (Business). Moscow, 1929.

# POETRY IN EXILE

As a consequence of the 1917 Revolution and several years of bloody civil war, Russian literature found itself split into two antagonistic camps —metropolitan and émigré. At the beginning of the 1920s the intellectuals, the cream of pre-Revolutionary culture, fled the country, mainly for Central and Western Europe. For more than half a century Russian literature has preserved this split, maintaining what Gleb Struve once called its "double life."

The two literatures, however, were never truly independent of each other. They were locked in a dialogue neither would end. Their relationship was particularly close immediately after the Civil War, when there was an overwhelming belief that Russian culture was still a single entity. Even in the mid-1920s it was not always easy to place a given writer securely in one camp or the other. In Berlin, which for a short time joined Moscow and Petersburg as a capital of Russian culture, some literary organizations embraced both émigrés and writers remaining in Soviet Russia, without regard for their political views.

## ■ *BERLIN*

The Berlin journal *Thing*, edited by the poet Ilya Erenburg and the avant-garde painter El Lissitzky, was a striking example of this consolidating tendency. Erenburg left Soviet Russia in 1921, emerging abroad as an ardent proponent of the achievements of Russian revolutionary art. His goal was to establish ties between avant-garde artists in Soviet Russia and in Europe. He wished to prove that despite catastrophe and deprivation, Russian culture was flourishing. The editors succeeded in attracting superb contributors to their cosmopolitan journal, which published original or translated materials in Russian, French, and German during its brief life (1922). There were poems by Mayakovsky, Pasternak, Esenin, and Aseev, by the French poets Charles Vildrac and André Salmon, and by the German expressionist Iwan Goll. Articles and notes by Khlebnikov, Kusikov, Valentin Parnakh, Aleksandr Tairov, Albert Gleizes, Theo van Doesburg, Fernand Léger, Gino Severini, Jacques Lipshitz, and Le Corbusier appeared in its pages.

все же, мог бы быть целесообразен. Однако писатели стремятся одновременно усвоить французские настроения и „точки зрения" не говоря уже про условности. Если они могли бы оставаться американцами (не в узком смысле этого слова) и приобрести французскую ясность и легкость выражения и стиля, было бы прекрасно, но писать плохие французские романы на хорошем английском языке — вряд ли имеет смысл. Парижская школа американской литературы могла бы принести большую пользу. Существует пропасть между Америкой и ее литературой. Это едва заметно на Восточном берегу Атлантического Океана, но вполне ясно на Западном. Пропасть, отделяющая представителей труда интеллектуального от мускульного, которая обособляет писателей, должна быть заполнена, если американская литература призвана перестать быть лишь внешним украшением. Великая литература всегда соответствует эпохе. Американская литература отражает лишь разбитые идеалы, угнетение полов, мелкую обыденщину. Наша цивилизация выше этого. Соприкосновение с французской мыслью должно поставить литературу в соответствии с цивилизацией. Сендрар и Фей — типичные представители наиболее сильной группы писателей послевоенного времени. Они отличаются от других тем, что узнали из личного опыта то, что другие узнают из рассказов. Оба жили и работали без денег и друзей в кошмарной обстановке промышленной борьбы, от которой содрогаются американские писатели. Им она нравилась. Работа американских литераторов для них лишена всякого интереса, тогда как естественные продукты нашей цивилизации кажутся им чудом века.

Эдмунд Вильсон — младший в журнале „Vanity Fair" старается защитить противоположную точку зрения; он обращается к Франции с предупреждением: „не играйте с машинами, смотрите, как бы эти слоны вас не задавили. Здания придавили нас, машины рвут нас на части. Наши идеалы выражены столбами с об'явлениями и джазом. Ваше стремление подражать варварству и грубости —

одно из самых ужасных явлений. Произведения дадаистов бледнеют перед электрическими рекламами Таим Сквера, — эти рекламы лучшее произведение дадаизма, естественно рожденное нашей расой, без той предумышленности, которая заставляет нас сознавать наши ужасы.

Г. Вильсон справедливо указал на недостатки американской интеллектуальности, хотя его толкование французского направления не вполне правильно:

„Здания нас придавили, машины рвут нас на части".

Нынешняя обстановка уже не та, что прежде. Человек должен был применяться к ней или быть выброшенным за борт. Практический человек не отставал от века и составляет сейчас одно целое с новым миром, сохранив при этом и свое здоровье. Мечтатель, идеалист из сентиментальности или по инерции и слабости остался позади и находится вне враждебного мира.

Он страдает и находит некоторое облегчение, изливая свою скорбь в печатном слове, что, впрочем, является радикальным терапевтическим средством, согласно психо-аналитической теории.

Многие американские писатели принадлежат к этой категории. Они напоминают скорее сбитого с ног пешехода, рассматривающего с интересом строение переехавшего его грузовика, нежели ученого, изучающего внутренний мир разоренного муравейника. Подобное положение неизменно влечет за собой с'уживание поля зрения.

Писатели предыдущего поколения впадали в противоположную крайность. Они были физически сильнее, но морально слабее. Марк Твэн является может-быть наиболее крупной фигурой этой эпохи. Никто никогда не сможет сказать, как велик был его гений, т. к. он подчинялся „моде", не сознавая насколько это сковывало его перо. Несмотря на то, что он все понимал — он описал лишь немногое. О'Хенри также знал Америку, но считался с ее предрассудками. Хотя в деталях он был правдивым, его философия

**ECOUTEZ, CANAILLES** ■ Cloués par ces lignes, ■ Restez muets ■ Ecoutez ces hurlements de loup ■ Qui ressemblent à peine à un poème! ■ Donnez ici ■ Le plus gros ■ Le plus chauve, ■ Prenez au collet et poussez le ■ Dans la boue et les comptes ■ Des Comités de l'aide aux affamés! ■ Regarde, ■ Tu vois ■ Derrière ces chiffres nus... ■ Un coup de vent ■ Fort et doux ■ Enveloppe dans la neige ■ Des milliers ■ De millions de toits, ■ La neige ■ Cercueil des villages du Volga. ■ Les cheminées, ■ Les cierges. ■ Même les corbeaux ■ Disparaissent, ■ Ils sentent ■ Que, fumante, ■ Arrive ■ Douce et nauséabonde, ■ L'odeur ■ Du fils, ■ Du père, ■ De la mère, ■ De la fille ■ Que l'on rôtit. ■ De qui est-ce le tour? ■ Il n'y aura pas de secours, ■ Séparés par la neige, ■ Pas de secours, ■ L'air est vide! ■ Pas de secours! ■ Sous les pieds, ■ Même le mortier ■ On le dévore! Même les mauvaises herbes! ■ Non, ■ Pas de secours, ■ Il faut se rendre. ■ Pour dix provinces ■ Mesurez les tombes. ■ Vingt millions ■ Vingt, ■ Couchez-vous, ■ Mourez! ■ Mais seule, ■ Avec une voix enrouée, ■ Avec de folles malédictions, ■ Les cheveux neigeux des chemins ■ Tirés par le vent, ■ Sanglote la terre. ■ Du pain, ■ Un peu de pain. ■ Encore du pain! ■ Elle même, voyant la mort en face, ■ Ayant à peine à manger, ■ Pour ne pas crever ■ La ville tend sa main ouvrière, ■ Une poignée de miette desséchées. ■ Du pain, ■ Un peu de pain, ■ Un peu de pain! ■ Les radio ■ Hurlent à toutes les frontières ■ Et comme réponse ■ Bêtises sur bêtises ■ Tombent dans les colonnes ■ Des journaux. ■ „Londres, ■ Banquet, ■ Présence du roi et de la reine ■ Qui bouffent ■ Ce qui ne pourrait rentrer ■ Dans une bauge tout en or!" ■ Soyez maudits! ■ Que ■ Pour votre tête couronnée ■ Des colonies ■ Accourent les sauvages ■ Les anthropophages, ■ Que ■ Brûle sur le royaume ■ L'incendie des révoltes! ■ Que ■ Vos capitales ■ Soient brûlées ■ Tout entières! ■ Que des princes héritiers ■ Des princesses, ■ Le manger ■ Se prépare ■ Dans des couronnes marmites! ■ „Paris, ■ Réunion du Parlement, ■ Rapport sur la famine ■ Par Fridjof Nansen". ■ On écoute en souriant ■ Comme un air de rossignol ■ Comme si on écoutait ■ Un ténor ■ Dans une romance à la mode. ■ Soyez maudits! ■ Que ■ Pour l'éternité ■ Vous n'entendiez plus ■ La voix humaine! ■ Prolétariat français ■ Hé! ■ Prends dans un noeud ■ Au lieu de discours, ■ Une foule de cous! ■ „Washington, ■ Les fermiers ayant bouffé, ■ Ayant bu, ■ Tellemnet ■ Qu'il leur faut ■ Une grue ■ Pour soulever leur panse! ■ Dans la mer ■ Ils jettent le superflu ■ De la fine farine, ■ Chauffent les locomotives ■ Avec du maïs!" ■ Soyez maudits! ■ Que ■ Vos rues ■ Soient pleines de révoltes, ■ Que, trouvant ■ Les places les plus sensibles, ■ Que le Nord ■ Et sur le Sud ■ De l'Amérique, ■ On joue de vos panses! ■ Comme des balles du foot-ball ■ „Berlin, ■ Les émigrés ressuscitent, ■ Leurs bandes sont satisfaites, ■ Avec les affamés ■ Ils se battent. ■ A Berlin, ■ Frisant sa moustache, ■ Marche, se vante, ■ Le patriote russe. ■ Soyez maudits! ■ Dehors! ■ Eternellemet! ■ Dégoûtez tout le monde ■ Par votre air de Judas, ■ Poursuivi par le son ■ De l'or français, ■ Soyez errants ■ Pour l'éternité! ■ Forêts russes, ■ Rassemblez-vous, ■ Choisissez vos plus grands arbres, ■ Que leur image ■ Toujours pendue, ■ Se balance toute bleue ■ Contre le ciel! ■ „Moscou, ■ La rassembleuse se plaint: ■ A l'Empire, ■ On fait des grimaces, ■ On y donne trente roubles ■ Qui ne marchent plus ■ Depuis 1918!" ■ Soyez maudits! ■ Que cela soit ainsi: ■ Que chaque bouchée avalée ■ Vous brûle l'estomac! ■ Qu'un biftek saignant ■ Se change en ciseaux ■ Et vous coupe les intestins! ■ Seront morts ■ Vingt millions d'hommes. ■ Au nom de tous ceux qui sont morts ■ Malédiction aujourd'hui ■ Jusqu'a l'éternité ■ A ceux qui ont détourné ■ Leur gueule bouffie ■ Du Volga! ■ Cette parole n'est pas ■ Pour la panse remplie ■ Ni pour le trône du Tsar! ■ Dans un tel coeur ■ Les mots ne peuvent rien toucher. ■ Les touchent ■ Les lances des révolutions! ■ A vous ■ Petits atomes ■ D'une énorme armée, ■ Avec la force de qui ■ Avec la force ■ Jetée dans les sous-sol, ■ On fera sauter le monde ■ Des milliardaires! ■ A vous! ■ A vous! ■ A vous! ■ Ces paroles-là! ■ Avec des chiffres kilomètriques ■ Faites le compte des bourgeois! ■ Le jour viendra ■ De l'incendie universel ■ Purifiant et fumant, ■ Mettant sans dessus dessous ■ Les palais des riches! ■ Soyez aussi. ■ Soyez sans pitié, ■ A cette heure ■ Du châtiment!

*Majakowsky.*

5

In the May issue Mayakovsky's poem "Svolochi" ("Dirty Scums") was published in a French translation by Tsvetaeva ("Écoutez, canailles"). The fact that Tsvetaeva and Mayakovsky stood on opposite sides of the political barricades lends particular poignancy to this publication. [124]

*Thing* was doomed, despite its quality, by the conservative artistic traditions already prevailing among the émigré intelligentsia. Most senior émigré writers opposed all modernist trends. The conservative or tradi-

■ *Item number 124*

**124** *Veshch* (Thing) 3 (May 1922).

On loan from The Hoover Institution

tionalist forces within émigré culture rallied around Ivan Bunin (1870-1953), the greatest of Russian writers in exile and the first Russian author to receive the Nobel Prize in literature (1933). His *Selected Poems*, published in 1929 by the émigré periodical, *Contemporary Annals*, showed his unwavering loyalty to nineteenth-century classical stylistic principles and his rejection of Symbolist and post-Symbolist novelties. [125]

The cult of Bunin in émigré literature appears clearly in the early writings of Vladimir Nabokov (1899-1977). In his review of Bunin's 1929 collection, Nabokov wrote: "The poems of Bunin are the best that have been created by the Russian Muse during the last several decades." Nabokov became known in Berlin's Russian literary circles in 1923 when, under the *nom de plume* V. Sirin, he published two collections of poetry, *The Cluster* and *The Imperial Path*. [126] Each contained a poem addressed to Bunin. Critics gave rather reserved evaluations of Nabokov as a poet, stressing his imitation of Bunin.

Nabokov joined the group of émigré writers who met at Gleb Struve's Berlin apartment and called themselves "The Round Table Fraternity." Besides Struve and Nabokov, the group included Sergey Krechetov, Ivan Lukash, Vladimir Amfiteatrov-Kadashev, Sergey Gorny, Leonid Strakhovsky [127], and the journalist Vladimir Tatarinov. An unsuccessful attempt was made to attract Marina Tsvetaeva and Aleksey Remizov. The minutes of the Fraternity's meetings preserved among Struve's papers contain a handwritten copy of an unpublished humorous poem by Nabokov. [128]

Dmitry Shakhovskoy (1902-), who left Russia in 1920, also owed much to Bunin. It was Bunin who encouraged his literary interests and introduced him to the literary circles of Russian Paris. Shakhovskoy's first book, *Poems*, came out in Paris in 1923. [129] Shakhovskoy spent the summer of 1924 with the Bunins in Grasse. Bunin was then writing his story "Mitia's Love," the published text of which is dedicated to Shak-

**125** IVAN BUNIN.
*Izbrannye stikhi* (Selected Poems). Paris, 1929.

This copy is inscribed by the author to Alexander Kaun (1899-1944), an American specialist in twentieth-century Russian literature. Kaun annotated his copy with translations of several of the poems.

**126** VLADIMIR NABOKOV.
*Gorny put* (The Imperial Path). Berlin, 1923.

**127** LEONID STRAKHOVSKY.
*U antikvara* (In the Antiquarian's Shop). Brussels, 1927.

This was published in a limited edition of 100 numbered copies. Strakhovsky inscribed this copy to Gleb Struve.

**128** Minutes of the Round Table Fraternity. Autograph manuscript.

On loan from The Hoover Institution

**129** DMITRY SHAKHOVSKOY.
*Stikhi* (Poems). Paris, 1923.

Shakhovskoy inscribed a dedicatory poem to Bunin in this copy.

■ *Item number 129*

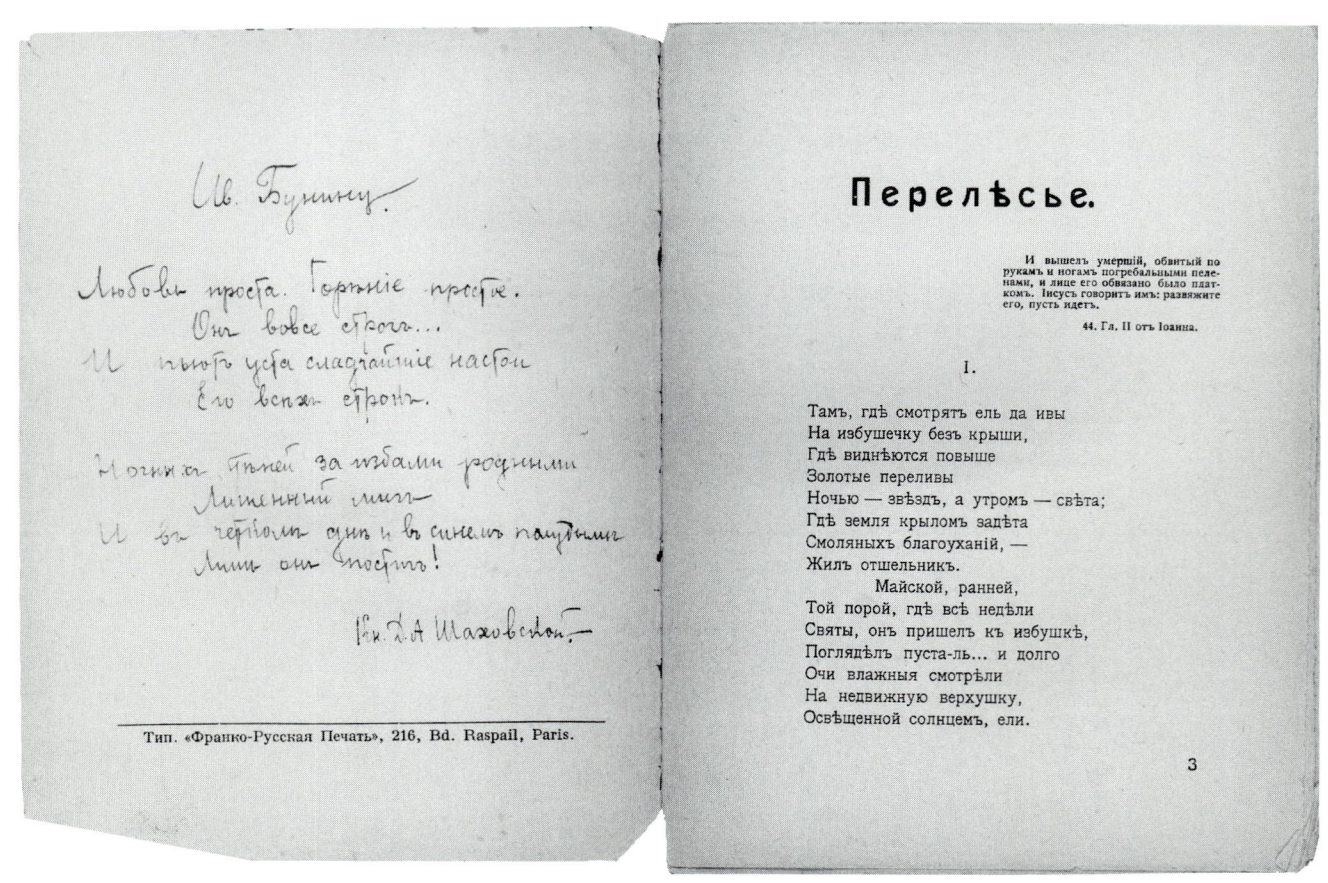

hovskoy. In the mid-1920s Shakhovskoy, by then the author of three verse collections, was on the verge of becoming one of the central figures of his literary generation. [130] His journal, *The Well-Intentioned One*, published in Brussels, managed to attract some of the best authors and critics active in émigré literature at the time, including Tsvetaeva and Dmitry Mirsky. Yet the deep spiritual crisis mentioned in his memoir, *The Story of My Youth*, led him to depart for Mount Athos, where he took monastic vows. Not until after the Second World War, when he became the Russian Orthodox Archbishop of San Francisco and the Western United States, did he resume his literary activity and publish several more books of poetry.

## ■ VLADISLAV KHODASEVICH

The traditionalist camp in Russian émigré poetry was represented also by the great poet Vladislav Khodasevich (1886-1939). First published in 1905, he was perceived as a somewhat anachronistic or peripheral figure until after the Revolution, when his two mature poetry collections, *Grain's Way* and *The Heavy Lyre*, were issued. [131] Their appearance marked a decisive return to Pushkinist traditions, a turning away from avant-garde principles.

Among the most enthusiastic admirers of Khodasevich's work was Gorky, then the undisputed leader of the politically independent artistic intellectuals in Petrograd. Gorky regarded Khodasevich's work as an antidote to the avant-garde trends that had plagued Russian literature since the turn of the century and were threatening to dominate post-Revolutionary cultural life.

**130** DMITRY SHAKHOVSKOY. *Predmety* (Things). Brussels, 1926.

This third book of Shakhovskoy's poems was published in a small edition and privately distributed to friends.

**131** VLADISLAV KHODASEVICH. *Tiazhelaia lira* (The Heavy Lyre). Berlin, 1923.

■ *Item number 132*

During the early period of the Civil War Khodasevich lived in Moscow and, like some of his colleagues, made his living by working at the bookshop operated by the Writers' Union. Besides printed books, this shop also sold, at special prices, a large number of manuscript booklets written and decorated by the authors. During the publishing freeze, these handwritten pamphlets became a symbol of the continuing vitality of literature. It was then that a manuscript booklet of Khodasevich's "Poems on a Tsar's Daughter" was produced. [132] The cycle contains five poems originally written in 1911 in Moscow and Genoa and included in his second poetry collection, *The Happy Little House* (1914).

Gorky had invited Khodasevich to join his publishing endeavors and insisted on his moving to Petrograd. During those years they became close friends. Their cooperation continued as they both, first Gorky and a year later Khodasevich, left for the West. In Berlin Khodasevich assisted Gorky in editing the periodical *Colloquy*, which was designed, like *Thing*, to bring together representatives of émigré and metropolitan culture. However, the political differences between the two men proved stronger than their friendship and their close ties were severed when they faced their final choice between personal independence and loyalty to Soviet Russia.

In exile Khodasevich worked on a new group of poems, "European Night." They never appeared under separate covers but were included in his collected poems in 1927. [133] He also became one of the most prolific and influential literary critics, his articles appearing mainly in the newspaper *Renaissance*. He was one of the two most influential mentors of younger émigré poets in Paris, along with Gumilev's former pupil Georgy Adamovich.

## ■ MARINA TSVETAEVA

If Khodasevich's poetry represented the conservative or neo-classical bent in émigré literature, Marina Tsvetaeva (1891-1941) represented its opposite, experimentalist bent. In this regard, her work was unique in the poetry of exile; none of the other major émigré poets even approached her audacious innovations in poetic technique and style. The metropolitan literature of the mid-1920s, though ostentatiously modernist in origins and orientation, proved to be less innovative than Tsvetaeva's work. Indeed, during these years Tsvetaeva emerged as the greatest poet of her generation. Mayakovsky, committed to political verses, had practically stopped writing lyrical poetry. Even Pasternak was experiencing the first symptoms of the deep artistic crisis that struck him in the 1930s.

Tsvetaeva's astounding growth as a poet coincided with her departure from Russia in the spring of 1922. It was strongly influenced by her reading of Pasternak's *My Sister, Life*. An ecstatic article on this book was her first attempt at critical prose. [134] From that moment until 1927 an intense dialogue in letters and poetry continued between her and Pasternak. Tsvetaeva's poems of that period were gathered in *After Russia*, her best collection and her last. [135] The present copy is inscribed to Ivan Bunin's wife, Vera Bunina (1881-1961), with whom Tsvetaeva had for some time carried on a lively correspondence, and to whom she dedicated her memoir, "The House Near Old St. Pimen's Church." [136, 137]

Russian émigré literature shows another striking example of a dramatic development of poetic artistry in exile—Georgy Ivanov (1894-1958). Ivanov, first published in 1911 as a member of the Ego-Futurist group, soon switched to the Poets' Guild. He contributed to the Acmeist collections and remained a devout pupil of Gumilev until the mid-1920s. [138, 139]

**132** VLADISLAV KHODASEVICH. "Stikhi o tsarevne" (Poems on a Tsar's Daughter). Autograph manuscript, September 20, 1920.

**133** VLADISLAV KHODASEVICH. *Sobranie stikhov* (Collected Poems). Paris, 1927.

**134** Marina Tsvetaeva to Aleksandr Iashchenko. Autograph letter signed. July 6, 1922.

On loan from The Hoover Institution

In her letter to Iashchenko, editor of the *New Russian Book*, Tsvetaeva discusses her plans to review Pasternak's book.

**135** MARINA TSVETAEVA. *Posle Rossii* (After Russia). Paris, 1928.

Signed by the author.

**136** Marina Tsvetaeva to Vera Bunina. Autograph letter signed. March 20, 1928.

On loan from The Hoover Institution

**137** MARINA TSVETAEVA. "Dom u Starogo Pimena" (The House Near Old St. Pimen's Church). Autograph manuscript.

On loan from The Hoover Institution

**138** GEORGY IVANOV. *Veresk* (Heather). Berlin, 1923.

Portrait of Ivanov by Yury Annekov.

**139** GEORGY IVANOV. *Sady* (Gardens). Petersburg, 1921.

Only abroad, with the appearance of his *Roses,* did he show his real worth and win wide recognition. [140, 141]

There were, of course, poets whose work—or influence—deteriorated in exile. Such was the case with Severyanin and Balmont, who continued to write in exile but never regained the earlier level of their poetic craft. The circle of poets connected with the Petrograd satirical journal *New Satiricon*—Sasha Cherny (1880-1932), Petr Potemkin (1886-1926), and Valentin Goriansky (1888-1944)-experienced a drastic loss of influence. Before 1917 their works not only were appreciated for themselves, but had tremendous influence on serious poetry. In the new cultural environment, satirical poetry was relegated to the entertainment section of the Sunday newspapers, and an abortive attempt to revive the *Satiricon* in Paris in 1931 could not rehabilitate the genre.

Valentin Goriansky (the penname of Valentin Ivanov) was the leading poet of *Satiricon*. His poems published there were reissued separately in 1915 as *Moi duraki* (My Fools). Goriansky welcomed the February Revo-

**140** GEORGY IVANOV. *Rozy* (Roses). Paris, 1931.

**141** GEORGY IVANOV. *Peterburgskie zimy* (Petersburg Winters). Paris, 1928.

Ivanov inscribed this copy to Peter Struve (1870-1944), a prominent political figure and editor of the newspaper *Vozrozhdenie* (Renaissance).

■ *Item number 137*

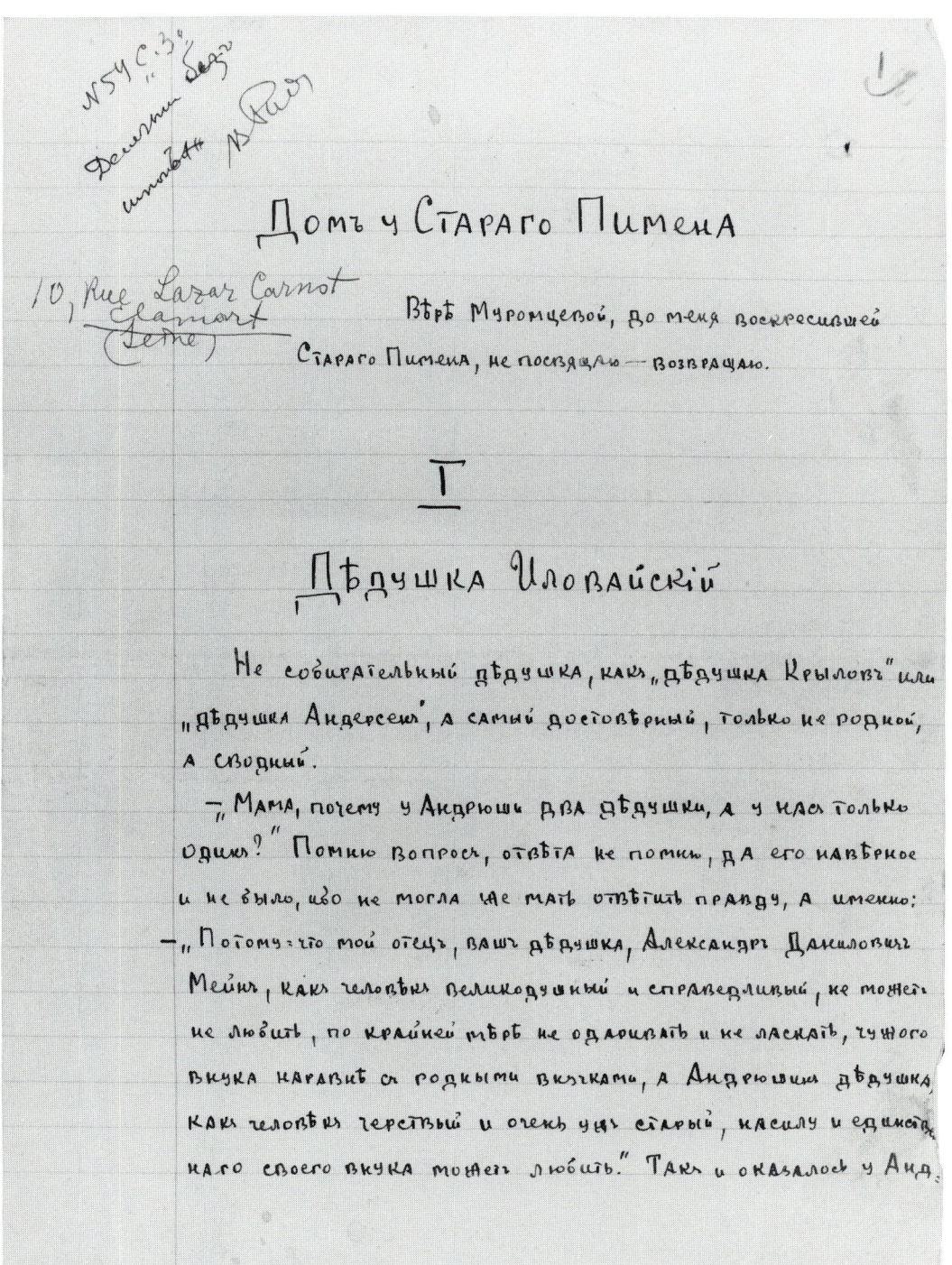

lution but rejected the Bolshevik order and emigrated in 1920. *Fiery Landmarks*, a poem on the Revolution, was published by Goriansky in a limited mimeograph edition during a stay in Constantinople in 1921. [142] He eventually settled in Paris. During the Second World War he collaborated with the Nazi occupation, for which he was ostracized by his compatriots. He died in 1944, almost completely forgotten.

### ■ PARIS

Wherever a younger generation of émigré writers emerged, the most interesting literary works and groups of the 1920s and '30s originated with them. One example was the shifting circle of young Russian poets led by Valentin Parnakh (1891-1951) in Paris in the 1920s. Having left Russia with little or no creative experience, they started their literary careers in a foreign linguistic and cultural environment. Especially interesting among them were Boris Bozhnev (1898-1969) [143], Aleksandr Ginger (1897-1965) [144], Boris Poplavsky (1903-1935), Dovid Knut (1900-1965), Vadim Andreev (1902-1976), Sergey Sharshun (1889-1975), and Dmitry Kobyakov. [145]

Parnakh stimulated their artistic activities at an early stage, while Russian cultural life in Paris was still dormant. Not until 1922 did Russian émigrés flock there in such numbers that Paris replaced Berlin as the foremost center of Russian culture in exile. Parnakh and his followers were striving for closer links between the young émigré poets and French artists and writers.

Parnakh made his literary debut in the early 1910s in Russia. He was one of the contributors to the Petersburg periodical *Love for Three Oranges*, edited by Vsevolod Meyerkhold, and devoted to theater and literature. He also participated in the poetry journal *Hyperboreus*, which was dominated by Acmeists.

In Paris, Parnakh, who had emigrated in 1915, was close to the colony of Russian artists. He also became acquainted with Picasso. All four of Parnakh's collections of poetry were published in Paris. In 1922 he decided to return to Soviet Russia. On his way back he sent an autobiographical sketch to the editor of the Berlin periodical *New Russian Book*, mentioning certain manuscripts as ready for publication. [146] None of them appeared in the Soviet Union, then or since, and to this day no one has uncovered them; as a poet, Parnakh had ceased to exist. Only his translations were printed from time to time in various Soviet and Western editions. He worked in Meyerkhold's theater in Moscow, became a "composer of dances," and introduced Russian audiences to jazz. [147]

### ■ EASTERN EUROPE AND THE FAR EAST

The decentralization of Russian literature abroad was one of its most important features. Along with Paris and Berlin, islands of Russian culture sprang up after the Revolution in Prague, Bucharest, Belgrade, Warsaw, Helsinki, Tallinn, Riga, Harbin, and Shanghai, as well as in Constantinople and in New York and San Francisco in the New World. Of course, the tenor and brilliance of Russian intellectual activities varied from city to city, depending on the size of the émigré colony and, in particular, on the prevailing economic and political conditions. Paris and Berlin were the best-known centers. However, the other outposts of Russian culture were by no means negligible. Many of the books published there were surprisingly free of provinciality. Conversely, the Parisian imprint did not guarantee artistic originality and significance.

The cultural life of Prague's Russian colony rivaled that of Paris in its

**142** VALENTIN GORIANSKY. *Vekhi ognennye* (Fiery Landmarks). Mimeograph. Constantinople, 1921.

**143** BORIS BOZHNEV. *Borba za nesushchestvovanie* (The Struggle for Non-existence). Paris, 1925.

**144** ALEKSANDR GINGER. *Predannost* (Faithfulness). Paris, 1925.

This copy is inscribed by the author to Mikhail Kantor, who worked with Georgy Adamovich on *Iakor* (Anchor), the anthology of émigré poetry.

**145** DMITRY KOBYAKOV. *Keramika* (Ceramics). Paris, 1925.

**146** Valentin Parnakh to Aleksandr Iashchenko. Autograph letter signed. ca.1922.

On loan from The Hoover Institution

In the discussion of his *The Acrobat is Clambering*, Parnakh discloses that two pages of the work were deemed pornographic by the publisher and were cut from the book.

**147** VALENTIN PARNAKH. *Karabkaetsia akrobat* (The Acrobat is Clambering). Paris, 1922.

intensity. In the 1920s it centered around one of the best émigré literary and political periodicals, *Freedom of Russia*, published there by the Socialist-Revolutionaries, with Tsvetaeva as one of its main contributors. Unlike the more conservative circle who published *Contemporary Annals* in Paris, the Prague group took a keen interest in novice émigré writers. The young Prague poets were strongly influenced in the 1920s by Tsvetaeva's and Pasternak's experiments in poetic form. Vyacheslav Lebedev (d.1969) was one of the most noteworthy representatives of this group. His only collection of verse, *The Astral Tilt*, was published in Prague in 1929. [148]

Although Russian cultural life was less visible in Poland than in Prague, some noteworthy developments took place in Warsaw, too. Above all should be mentioned the book *Arion: About the New Poetry Abroad*, written by the poet, prose writer, and literary critic Lew Gomolicky (Leon Gomolicki, b.1903), who began writing entirely in Polish after World War II. [149] *Arion* was the first survey of the works of young émigré poets. [150] Both as a scholarly work and as an eye-witness account, it has not lost its significance even today, more than half a century after its publication.

**148** VYACHESLAV LEBEDEV.
*Zvezdny kren* (The Astral Tilt). Prague, 1929.

Inscribed by the author to Gleb Struve.

**149** LEW GOMOLICKY.
"Edinoborets" (The Lonely Fighter). Autograph manuscript. August, 1924.

Gomolicky also illustrated this manuscript poem, which was written in prose form with regular rhymes.

**150** LEW GOMOLICKY.
*Arion: O novoj zarubezhnoj poezii* (Arion: About the New Poetry Abroad). Paris, 1937.

Inscribed by the author to Dmitry Merezhkovsky

■ Item number 147

At one point, Harbin was second only to Paris as a center of Russian culture abroad. After the defeat of the Whites in Siberia and the Russian Far East, the Russian population of this junction on the Manchurian Railway soared to about 200,000. There were theaters and libraries, several Russian-language daily newspapers, a weekly paper called *Borderline*, publishing and printing houses. There were also several young writers, among whom Arseny Nesmelov (the penname of A. Mitropolsky; 1891-1945) stood out as the most talented, original, and prolific.

Nesmelov started his literary career as a prose writer shortly before World War I. A Muscovite by birth and education, he came to Siberia in 1918 to join Admiral Kolchak's White Army. In Siberia he met Aseev and Tretyakov, who convinced him to pursue a poetic vocation and encouraged him to publish his verses. In Vladivostok two of his first lyrical books, *Poems* and *Ledges*, were published, as well as his long poem "Tikhvin." [151, 152] In 1925 he moved to Harbin, but his thoughts still turned to Siberia. *The Bloody Gleam* [153], a book of poems recounting the events of the Civil War in Siberia, was published in Harbin in 1928, and he continued to contribute to the Soviet periodical, *Siberian Lights*. His poetry shows striking affinity with the poetic styles of Mayakovsky, Aseev, and Tsvetaeva.

In the 1930s Nesmelov became a sympathizer of the Russian Fascist Party in Harbin, and wrote some of the poems used as lyrics for the offi-

**151** ARSENY NESMELOV.
*Stikhi* (Poems). Vladivostok, 1921.

In Nesmelov's first book of poetry, the poem "Oboroten" (Werewolf) is dedicated to Mayakovsky.

**152** ARSENY NESMELOV.
*Ustupy* (Ledges). Vladivostok, 1924.

**153** ARSENY NESMELOV.
*Krovavy otblesk* (The Bloody Gleam). Harbin, 1928.

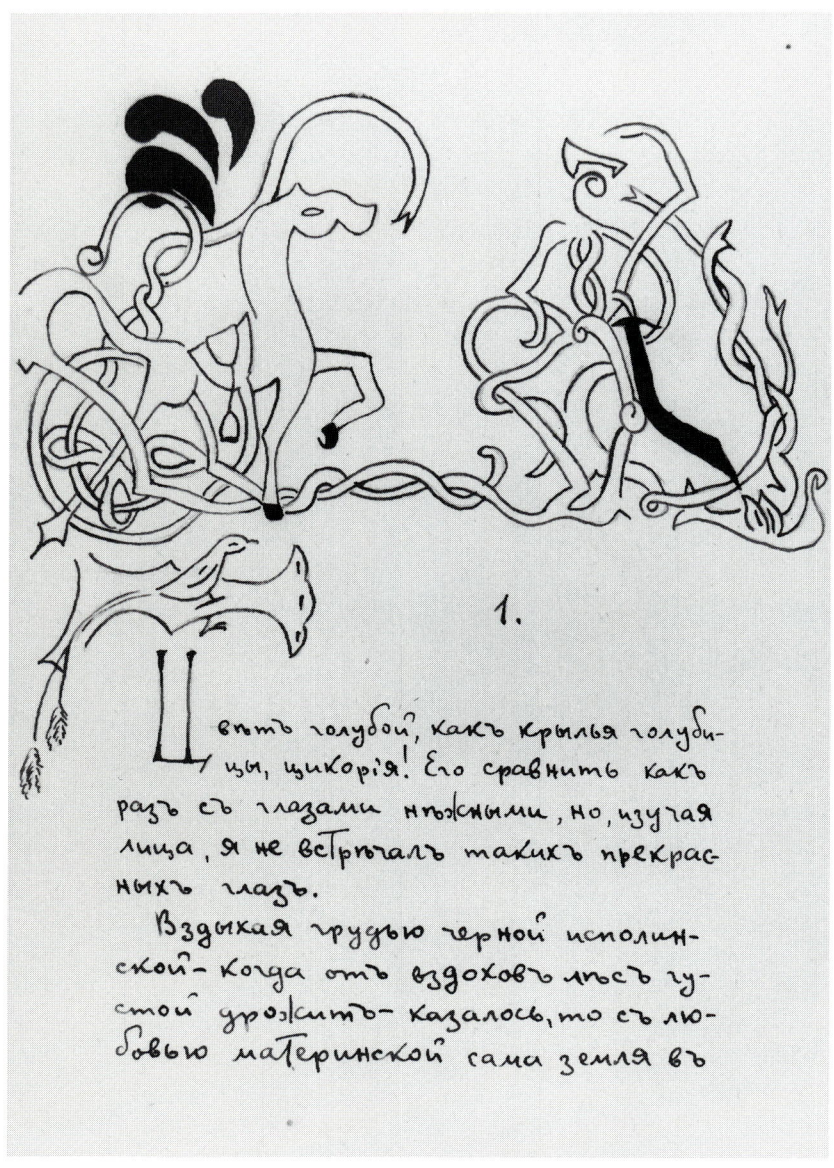

■ *Item number 149*

cial Party hymns. Immediately after the Soviet Army occupied Manchuria in August 1945, he was arrested and reportedly died on his way to a concentration camp in Siberia. The first inklings of his literary rehabilitation have just appeared in the Soviet press, as part of a general reevaluation of the émigré literary heritage made possible by *perestroika*.

Russian poetry of the early twentieth century is a unique phenomenon not only in its diversity of poetic schools and styles, and its complex relationships with contemporary artistic and political trends, but also in its "posthumous" fate. Between the 1930s and the 1950s its entire heritage was deliberately neglected in the Soviet Union. Indeed, the Soviets tried to obliterate it from collective memory as if this period had never existed or had no claim to public interest. Now the poetry of the Silver Age is experiencing its "second birth," with the profound and comprehensive reexamination and reappraisal evident in recent works published both in Russia and elsewhere. Our Stanford exhibition is a modest attempt to further these studies.